AN EXTRAORDINARY BUSINESS
The story of James Martin Associates

AN EXTRAORDINARY BUSINESS

The story of James Martin Associates

Andrew Crofts

McGRAW-HILL BOOK COMPANY

London · New York · St Louis · San Francisco · Auckland
Bogotá · Caracas · Hamburg · Lisbon · Madrid · Mexico
Milan · Montreal · New Delhi · Panama · Paris · San Juan
São Paulo · Singapore · Sydney · Tokyo · Toronto

Published by
McGRAW-HILL Book Company (UK) Limited
Shoppenhangers Road, Maidenhead, Berkshire, SL6 2QL, England
Telephone 0628 23432
Fax 0628-35895

British Library Cataloguing in Publication Data

Crofts, Andrew
    An extraordinary business : the story of James Martin
    Associates.
    1. Computer services. Consultancy
    I. Title
    004.068

ISBN 0-07-707311-8

Library of Congress Cataloging-in-Publication Data

Crofts, Andrew
    An extraordinary business : the story of James Martin
    Associates / Andrew Crofts.
        p. cm.
    ISBN 0-07-707311-8
    1. James Martin Associates. 2. Information services industry-
-Great Britain. 3. Business consultants—Great Britain. I. Title.
HD9999.I494J353   1990
338.7'61001'0941—dc20   90-33082

12345BS 93210

Typeset by Clifford-Cooper Ltd, Aldershot
and printed and bound in Great Britain by Billing and Sons Ltd Worcester

CONTENTS

Preface

1	'Showtime'	1
2	The captain's name was Carter	11
3	An urge to change the world	19
4	Planning a new corporation	21
5	The odd couple	27
6	Mission critical	39
7	Early days	47
8	Bermuda—the birthplace of CASE	61
9	The consultancy grows	69
10	Becoming multinational	87
11	Shootout at Mooselips	105
12	America	111
13	Texas Instruments and the IEF	121
14	'Fairbrain'	135
15	The financial minefield	145
16	The big launch	155
17	Winning more business	161
18	The winning formula	167
19	Fast forward into the future	173

PREFACE

This is the story of an extraordinary business, and the title applies at two different levels.

First, it is the story of a consulting company which has grown from nothing to an annual turnover of £25 million in just eight years.

Second, it is the story of the industry in which this company works, the high-technology field. Both these businesses are extraordinary. There has never been anything like them before, and the effect which they are having on the business world is massive.

It is a revolution, and the changes which will result from it are as far-reaching as those brought about by the Industrial Revolution a century ago.

The Industrial Revolution changed the world. It created gigantic cities and drained the countryside of people. It lifted the average standard of living within the Western world beyond anything that could have been dreamt of two hundred years ago. It made us what we are today. Whether you like the results or not, they are unavoidable. We now have factories, cars, aeroplanes, space shuttles, and enough food for everyone (the inefficient distribution of this food is another question).

The impetus for all this change came from the worlds of trade and commerce. Trade provided the money which built the bridges and roads, which made the distribution possible, that created the products that built the companies...and so the song goes on.

Today the great traders, now mostly in the form of giant global companies, are forcing the pace of change once more. This time they are using information and controlling it on an incredible scale. The investment going into the high-technology industries, coupled with the complexity of the subject, has led to an emergence of a new elite, made up of the people who know how to create systems which make these developments possible.

Whereas in the past it was the people who built railroads and mined for precious metals who were able to grow rich, it is now the people who know how to control and distribute knowledge who hold the key to future wealth.

Knowledge is now the most important commodity in the world. Everyone needs it, but only a few people know how to provide it in sufficient quantities and in useful forms. Only a few people know how to extract the nuggets of gold from all the surrounding dirt, and deliver them to the right people at the right times.

This is the story of one such set of people, working on the teachings of one of the most successful gurus ever.

Most of the main characters in the story started working in the 1960s, when the computing industry was in its infancy, and when there was little in the way of structured career paths to follow. They came from diverse places, but all of them shared a fascination with something which was new and unknown, something which they all believed would one day change the world.

The story also shows how a consulting company works, how they gain credibility in the marketplace, how they recruit their people, sell their services and manage their projects, how they go out into the international markets and set up a global operation.

.How do a group of people decide one day that they are going to be the best consultancy in the high-technology market, and then go out and convince the biggest and most sophisticated companies in the world that this is a fact? It is indeed an extraordinary business.

'SHOWTIME'

PREPARING FOR THE FUTURE

- Every successful business needs a good product, but that product might simply be the people or their ideas.

- Every successful business must understand the marketplace and be able to identify extraordinary opportunities.

- A successful business must try to understand and predict the future, otherwise it is depending on luck alone.

- Everyone wants to buy information and wisdom. People who manage to acquire these can virtually name their price.

- The future is the greatest potential marketplace the world has ever seen.

It is a blustery autumn evening in Britain. The lights from the glass-fronted office foyer spill out on to the newly laid, red-brick forecourt. Inside, a string quartet is making light, formal music. Outside, uniformed chauffeurs chat in small groups, leaning on expensive, shiny company cars, waiting for their employers to emerge from the building and head home for the weekend.

A waiting taxi driver is talking into his radio; 'There's some ''do'' on here,' he says, as the crowd of suited figures moves through the galleried reception area towards the champagne reception being prepared in other rooms.

The guests are walking in small groups, clutching folders of information, discussing the performance which they have just witnessed and perhaps dancing around the edges of talking business. It would be impossible for an outsider to differentiate between the few truly powerful corporate figures in the crowd, and the people whose brains they have come to pick. Everyone looks the same and they are all there for similar reasons. They are there to look into the future, hoping to see some signposts of where they should go if they are to survive and prosper in a fast-changing commercial jungle, where one wrong decision can cost millions and can lead a company to losing a hard-won competitive edge. They have also come to be excited and inspired by the possibilities before them. They have come to be sold solutions to problems, and to discover keys which will unlock incredible riches. They have come to see a 'show'.

It is just as easy for senior business people to become bogged down in the mundane details of day-to-day survival as ordinary mortals, and to ignore the broader pictures. We all tend to fall into the trap of allowing ourselves to dissipate our energies on fire-fighting and tactical problem-solving, not leaving ourselves time to form strategic plans and goals which we can build slowly and steadily towards, while at the same time dealing with the day-to-day distractions which arise along the way.

It is tempting for all of us to fall into the trap of seeing only problems before us and of drawing only negative conclusions. With the right teachers, however, it is sometimes possible to reverse old ways of thinking and old ways of doing things, and suddenly to see the way forward with blinding clarity. Henry Ford saw the future when he first mass-produced the motor car. In the high-technology area, Steve Jobs envisaged a world where everyone would have a personal computer, at a time when no one knew what the term meant. His was a broad, visionary dream. Alan Sugar saw the future in a more down-to-earth way when he created Amstrad for a marketplace which then didn't exist. All of them had visions of the future, rooted in optimism. Their creations grew to fulfil their own prophesies. Tonight the crowd of business people are there both to listen to a teacher who paints a broad picture of the future, and to consider the practical details of how to achieve the growth and rewards which he forsees as possible. They want to ensure that they get a piece of the action, and are not left behind by competitors who knew something they didn't.

The office block stands in Ashford, a suburb south of London which must once have been a rural village, but which is now a sprawl of low-income housing beside one of the main motorway arteries into the capital city. It is a grey, monotonous area where nobody is too poor, but nobody has quite enough.

But the future involves everyone. In the small houses surrounding the office, colour televisions are flickering, ready and able to receive the satellite channels that will soon be beaming down over the whole globe. People are talking on cordless telephones, listening to compact discs, and playing with home computers. The high-technology and communications revolution has been working its way into their lives gradually for twenty years, without them even realizing that it is changing everything they do.

If they look out of their windows at the illuminated foyer opposite they will just see a group of business people talking. They have no idea just how fast things are going to be changing. Some of them may have lost jobs through automation, many of them will have retrained in new skills, and adapted to their changing circumstances, but the changes they have experienced so far are nothing compared to the whirlwind which is coming. High-technology is a powerful engine; until now it has just been idling, but someone has just pushed the accelerator to the floor.

The business people inside the office block have an idea of what is coming. They have just received a hurricane warning and they are now trying to work out how to ensure that the lives of their families, employees and customers are not swept away in the winds of change.

In the competitive world of modern international business, no one can afford to be behind the times any more. If one bank introduces a plastic debit card, all the others must follow suit. If one major airline introduces a system for automatic booking those that don't follow will soon be out of business. Technical excellence may lead to fast results on the bottom line, but only after vast sums of money have been invested—or risked—on investigating the possibilities for change.

Everyone has come to recognize that the most powerful weapon in any competitive situation, from global warfare to big business, from police work to microchip research, is information. With the right information you can achieve everything; without it you can achieve nothing. Information in this context is now more generally known as data, and everyone needs to build a bigger and more accurate database than the competition. Once they have built them they need to be able to manage them effectively in order to achieve the right results. They need computer software which is created with their special needs in mind. They need help.

At the same time the people within the big corporations, who must decide how to invest for the future, are aware that costly mistakes can be made by organizations that move too fast. It is always expensive being a pioneer in any business. It is a gamble which more often than not fails to pay off, but those who do win (like Henry Ford and Steve Jobs) reap massive rewards. In order to hedge their bets, the wise company leaders need information on what everyone else is doing, so that they can be ready with their own answer to every challenge. They don't want to spend millions of pounds on research and development which will prove fruitless and will divert them from other activities. But new products are being developed in the high-technology areas every day, each one with more and different capabilities to its predecessors. If you invest today, your system might be rendered obsolescent tomorrow. If you don't invest today you might be out of business tomorrow.

The decision-makers are walking a tightrope between success and failure. Anyone who can help them to keep their balance, or who can just talk them safely through to the end of the wire, is worth listening to. If there are answers for sale, and the salespeople can convince the customers that they are likely to be effective, then they are worth any amount of money.

The string quartet in the foyer plays on, almost unnoticed, sitting underneath the open-plan staircase which leads up to the first-floor gallery. On the wall above the staircase, curtains have been pulled back to reveal a portrait, double life size, of an evangelical figure. He is a man in his middle age, with his arms open in a gesture of explanation and welcome.

On the other side of the foyer is a twenty-foot-high, stained-glass sculpture, incorporating some esoteric letters — IEF, TI, JMA, TM, IEM. They all mean a great deal to the assembled crowd below. There is also an image which looks like the blue seas surrounding Bermuda, and a mixture of international flags incorporated into the design.

The portrait above the stairs, with hands outstretched, seems to be guiding people into a world of globalization and infinite possibilities. The man is Dr James Martin, and it is his teachings and writings which have tempted the audience to give up a Friday afternoon in order to watch him, and possibly to meet him. Within the computing industry his reputation is legendary. A recent poll by a leading magazine indicated that 93 per cent of people within the computer industry accepted him as their most influential guru. The outside world, however, is less aware of his activities.

The office belongs to James Martin Associates (JMA), a consulting company which has been created to pick up the teachings of this inventor of information engineering, and carry them forward into the future. It is a company which—to quote a well-known journalist in the computing field—'simply oozes brains'.

James Martin himself is an international figure, who hob-nobs with presidents and kings and commands fees of $25,000 a day for consulting work and seminar appearances. He is here this evening to ensure a good turnout for the official opening of JMA's new office in Ashford.

The opening event has cost the company £20,000, but no one is complaining. The secrets of a good teacher are clarity, simplicity and communication. Anything that helps to inspire confidence in the audience, and ensures that they listen closely to what is being said, is worth doing. Like most good teachers, James Martin is a showman. He enjoys performing. He likes to shock his audiences with facts and projections about how life and business will be in the predictable future, and he aims to send them away fired with enthusiasm, floating on a cloud of adrenalin which will lead to action. The secret of his success is that he is able to generate excitement about subjects which most people find a bore and a necessary evil. He has been able to 'turn on' top management to computing, at the very highest levels.

He talks about microelectronics and genetic engineering. He tells of chips doubling their capacity every year and a half and of the development of chips with networks of neurons, like the neurons in the human brain. He explains how small silicon chips are being replaced by large chips and ultimately wafers, and how new technology chips are working at far higher speeds. He awakens his audience to the possibilities of worldwide networks linking millions of computers, of microbiology, robots and mass-production factories operating largely without workers. He talks about optical fibres which can transmit the whole of Shakespeare in a quarter of a second and computers for artificial intelligence 10,000 times faster than those of today.

To illustrate his points, and to make them understandable to the audience, he describes the possible social consequences of these developments in terms of unemployment and a widening division between 'them and us'. He makes predictions like the production of the cost of 100-kiloton nuclear bombs falling to $100,000, and then sketches out the implications for world peace. He can move seemingly effortlessly between subjects, able to create patterns which link Star

Wars defence systems with satellite television, nuclear fusion and population explosions.

The show was staged in a clear frame structure flown in specially from Holland and built on to the side of the office block, over the rear car park. Inside it is like a sophisticated discothèque. During the show lights flashed and popped, audiovisual images flickered, expanded and faded, clouds of dry ice billowed over the stage and James Martin appeared, an evangelist of change.

He had arrived in England only hours before and the marketing people had been slaving long nights over a new audiovisual show to illustrate his thinkings. Minutes before he appeared from the smoke he decided to do without the mechanical aids. He couldn't get the six linked projectors to work smoothly for him. The greatest proponent of technology is relying on the old-fashioned communication methods of speech and gesture. He is confident that he can deliver the whole show from memory. His staff, who are tense with pre-show nerves and exhausted from their preparations and rehearsals, are horrified at the last-minute changes, but he is about to go on-stage to do a show, so everyone has to put a brave face on it. He is the reason everyone is there. Everything goes smoothly, as Martin knows it will. The audience has no idea that anything is amiss. It is a piece of pure showbusiness — the show must go on.

The show has been directed by a man who made his reputation directing pop concerts. Video cameras cover every angle and still cameras click and whirr each time James Martin makes one of his characteristic, expansive gestures.

He talks fast, punching ideas, facts and figures out quickly. Martin is one of the most expensive speakers in the world, so he must give value for money. A decade earlier one of his predictions was that the world's top teachers would eventually make as much money as top film stars. He is one of the few teachers who has been able to make this particular prediction come true.

When he gives seminars outside the English-speaking world the translators are only able to work in 15-minute shifts, due to the high pressure of his delivery. He paints a picture of how life is going to be for all of us. He produces statistics which are impossible to remember but which give an impression to the audience of just how fast things are changing. He drops in little pieces of information which he has picked up from the top brass and brightest boffins of the biggest high-technology and computer companies in the world. He shows that he not only knows what is happening, but understands all the implications.

James Martin was introduced on to stage by Tony Carter, a rugby player with irrepressible charm and a face moulded by a thousand scrums. At the time Tony Carter was Martin's partner and the managing director of JMA. If the teachings and philosophies of James Martin are to outlive the man, if they are to be made real and spread widely, it will be because JMA is building a formidable international consultancy at a speed almost as dazzling as the changes which Jim predicts.

In August 1987 the Board of JMA set corporate objectives for 1988 of £16 million in revenue, with pre-tax earnings of £1.4 million. In fact the company produced a revenue of £20.2 million and pre-tax earnings of £1.49 million. It was an 80 per cent revenue growth and a 420 per cent increase in earnings on the previous year. It gave the company an average revenue per employee of more than £70,000.

Having started from nothing with very little capital in 1981, the company is growing at around 100 per cent a year, evolving from an entrepreneurial start-up, flying by the seat of its pants from one job to the next, into a major force in the consulting world. The speed of the growth makes it look as if the rise has been smooth but, as every entrepreneur knows, there is no such thing as easy success. Along the way the company has had several close brushes with collapse, and has faced all the painful struggles of raising money, generating cashflow, recruiting the best people and developing products which the world would want to buy.

Even as he speaks on stage, there are internal, political rumblings which threaten the position of the colourful Tony Carter. The man who starts a successful company isn't always the best person to run an established operation and even Tony had begun to question whether he was the appropriate leader to take JMA into the future. Confrontation has been his style all through his career. It has made many people admire him, but just as many who would rejoice at his downfall and would encourage his departure from the controlling position at JMA.

Twenty years ago hardly anyone in the world knew what software was. Computers were huge pieces of machinery which had to be kept in expensive, air-conditioned rooms in company basements, eating up money and filling their owners with apprehension and loathing. Since then there has been a revolution. Pioneers like Steve Jobs at Apple and powerful corporations like IBM have created a whole new world, and a generation of computer-literate people have grown up and reached positions of influence. Technology, like the human brain, is always capable of delivering far more than it is ever called upon to prove. Now, however, as we enter the last decade of the twentieth century, all the disparate pieces of the jigsaw are coming together. Developments in telecommunications and broadcasting technology, coupled with massive increases in computer power and in the willingness of people to use it, mean that things are now going to change very fast indeed.

When Henry Ford demonstrated that it was possible to make cars at an affordable price, there were still no major road networks. There was no comprehensive infrastructure for repairing or refuelling the machines. People could see the recreational possibilities of owning their own cars, but they could not possibly see that it would lead to a complete change in our lifestyles, to the growth of motel chains, out-of-town shopping malls, and a travel industry which would cover everything from Disney World to the Golden Gate Bridge. From the back streets of Calcutta to the autobahns of West Germany, the motor car has altered everything, and now high-technology will change it all again.

Early futurologists, like George Orwell, saw nothing but bad coming from the spread of technology. James Martin sees the opposite side of the coin. Far from being a means of repression, he sees technology as a means of freeing humankind from unnecessary toil, and of creating a utopian way of life for all. Rather than just looking at the 'means' by which things are achieved such as technology, law, management, politics, programming and profit-making, he encourages audiences to think of the 'ends', which relate to the ways in which people enjoy the fruits of their labours.

Instead of creating work for its own sake, he believes that a highly civilized society concentrates on the ultimate purposes of their labours and minimizes the drudgery needed to get there. Technology, he points out, will remove that drudgery and create wealth. Not only does it give people superb hi-fi and television systems, it also provides access to knowledge and computerized logic. Electronic technology can lower ecological damage and aid the 'green' revolution. It gives mobility and is creative, making possible the machinery of film-making and theatre.

His wider dreams for mankind may still be a long way in the future, but he has shown that the first practical steps can and are being taken by the powers which run the richest governments and corporations of today.

In two hours James Martin cannot go into too much detail with his audience. He paints a broad picture of what is possible. If they want to turn his images into reality they will have to come to his detailed, frantically fast-paced, five-day how-to-do-it seminars, or hire large quantities of practical, hands-on assistance from JMA.

Martin understands more than most the need for man to escape from the high-pressured world of modern technology to recharge his batteries. Although he is famous for his futuristic thinkings on the telecommunications industry he retreats to places where the telephones don't work to write his voluminous textbooks, or to create meticulously detailed computerized methodologies. In one of his mountain retreats he has a theatre with five screens, seven computers, a media room with television editing devices, computer-controlled laser-discs and six channels of hi-fi, but when he wrote *Information Systems Manifesto*, one of the most influential books in the industry, he was working in a cottage on a remote New Zealand sheep station, which could be accessed only by helicopter, and which was heated by one log fire.

To keep up with him and his ideas, the executives of JMA and their clients often have to be prepared to visit his hideouts to conduct workshops about how to make it all work.

THE CAPTAIN'S NAME WAS CARTER

EVERY DISASTER IS AN OPPORTUNITY

- How being fired can make you more successful, and the making of an entrepreneur in an immature marketplace.

- Walking away from everything can serve to demonstrate how easily it can all be won back if you have the right attitude—and how easily you can walk away again.

- Every entrepreneur has to serve an apprenticeship. The harder that apprenticeship is, the tougher the entrepreneur will be at the end. Steel is created by subjecting it to enormous heat and beating the hell out of it with hammers.

- To be successful an entrepreneur must know where to go for the best talent, and be able to persuade the best talent to play on the team.

On Friday, 15 May 1981 Dr William Fain, the American President of CACI, boarded Concorde. He was heading for London to fire Tony Carter, his European Chief Executive, and a man he himself had hired.

Tony Carter had set up CACI in London in 1975. The company was doing well, growing at a steady rate, building a reputation as a leading player among European database consultancies, with its own particular market niche. It was a small company doing challenging things with the development of database methodologies. It was a company with a future, and it was making a lot of money.

Tony is an entrepreneur. A solid Cornishman with a face chiselled in granite and a passion for rugby. He sees the business world as analogous with the sports field. He is a team leader, playing ferociously hard to win and enjoying the game. He is deceptively quietly spoken at one moment, and ferociously confrontational at another. His friends say he is a brilliant 'people manager'. His enemies say he is arrogant and autocratic. Above all else he is a salesman. He enjoys nothing more than taking a new product and building a business out of it. He is full of ideas and always impatient to see them all come to fruition. The software industry has been a fertile growing area for such entrepreneurs, because it has grown so fast from nothing, and because it offers almost unlimited potential.

The computing industry is full of inventors with exciting ideas, dedicated enthusiasts who will work all the hours they can just for the love of their subject. These people are seldom good business people, and without help their ideas often founder and fail, not because they were bad ideas, but because they were badly managed. Any strong leaders, who are able to take the products which these people create and apply rigorous business principles to their development and marketing, can build successful businesses quickly.

Not that strong leadership guarantees success. There were times during the growth of JMA when Tony's bombastic approach did more harm than good. When a company is growing fast, however, it is better to have someone who is willing to take decisions and risks; that is what gives small companies an advantage over larger ones which have to move more slowly and cautiously.

Anything that grows quickly is bound to be less stable than something which has taken decades to mature. If the mighty organizations of the world are the old oak trees in the business forests, these young companies are quick-growing conifers which, if they don't meet with any catastrophes along the way, can in time grow to be as tall and strong as the existing oaks. The entrepreneurs, therefore, also have to be strong enough to hold their young saplings upright when the strong winds start to blow, winds that would do no more than rustle the leaves of an established oak tree.

In any immature marketplace there is bound to be some natural wastage at the beginning. There will be the ideas which looked good on the drawing board but did not prove practical in reality. There are the good ideas which come just too late, finding themselves upstaged at the last moment by someone else's even better idea. Many of the early companies came and went with alarming speed. Others prospered enormously and were sold quickly to larger, less adventurous operations, allowing their founders to move on to new things, or to retire in comfort.

As the market matures the sheep have had to separate out from the goats. The customers now have a better idea of what it is they need, and the suppliers are infinitely better at giving it to them. It is no longer quite such a haphazard game of chance. Precedents are set and rules formed, which make the chances of expensive failures less, but make the odds against coming up with something radically new higher. Tony Carter had been in the industry throughout these changes.

He set up his first business, at the age of thirty, in 1969 having worked at several jobs before, including a stint as a cartoonist. The company which he formed was called Computer Co-operatives, and marketed US software packages following the announcement by IBM that they were unbundling in 1968. He was one of the first people to set out, as he described it, 'carpet-bagging' in America and negotiating software marketing contracts for Europe. These were pioneering days for software marketing, and Tony was one of the founders of the International Software Products Association. The Association tried to form a cartel which could dictate in the US what the terms were for marketing packages in Europe.

Computer Co-operatives was before its time and did not prosper as greatly as Tony felt it should. As in many pioneering situations, everything which they were predicting would happen, did, but it took far longer to get the message across to the marketplace than they had expected. Tony sold out to a Scottish computer services company in 1973. He was confident that he could be a successful entrepreneur and he now knew that the software industry was the one he wanted to stay in, but he needed to find a way of building a more substantial business. One way to start something solid was to find someone who would back him, and would give him a foundation stone on which to build.

In December 1975 CACI was advertising for entrepreneurs to set up business units for them in Europe. At that time CACI was a $7 million US computer consultancy. They were a publicly owned company, quoted on the New York Stock Exchange. They were heavily into government work in America and felt that the time was right to expand their business philosophies into other countries. Europe was an obvious target market, but they needed to find someone on the spot to set up the business, rather than trying to do it with expatriate Americans. The company was destined to become a database consultancy, since there seemed to be a gap in the market for people who knew about database technology and understood the possibilities for the future. The company has some very set ideas on how to build and run successful operations, all of which impressed Tony.

He came up with a business plan explaining how he would handle the job, presented it to them on a Saturday and was given the job on the Monday, with CACI agreeing to provide the back-up. In the beginning he just took on the UK market, but his success quickly led to his spreading his operations across most of continental Europe. Building the business was up to him. First he had to do the selling, and then ensure that he could provide the services he was promising. CACI had provided him with administrative back-up, with their name and their corporate culture, but they had given him no equity. He learnt a number of invaluable lessons. He learnt how to build a successful business from scratch, how to sell, how to recruit and how to manage. He learnt that the database market was still in its infancy, but that it had unlimited promise for the future. He discovered that international borders did not have to act as barriers if you could find the right people to straddle them. He also built up a team of experts and a network of industry contacts which would prove to be his most valuable assets in the long term.

At the time of setting up CACI, database methodologies were largely unknown, although they were being worked on in various companies, and Tony simply had a feeling that people were using the technology to do something interesting. He began to build a team from a diversity of backgrounds with the intention of building the best database group in the world. Another part of CACI in Europe was providing market research and analysis and the whole group grew to become a catalyst for the database industry of the 1980s. Fifteen years after the formation of CACI Europe, the companies which have split off and grown independently under the initial team members now represent a considerable market force. It was the beginning of an industry, and most of the people who were going to be important to the movement were drawn to that first company.

As well as building and managing the company, Tony also occasionally had to bill himself out as a consultant, teacher and lecturer. He was proud of the job he was doing. Within just over five years the part of the European operation under him had grown to 200 people and billings of $8 million. The group as a whole had grown from $7 million to $60 million.

Such a good rate of growth had not come without costs. Tony's twenty-year marriage to his wife Pat was in trouble, strained by many years of separation through work, and by Pat's dislike of the business-travelling lifestyle.

When William Fain told Tony he was flying over on that Friday afternoon, and invited him to the Dorchester Hotel for breakfast 'to discuss the figures', Tony felt only the faintest whiff of discomfort.

The trees in Park Lane were in full spring leaf, and Tony felt hungry on the way to the meeting. Fain seemed affable and Tony ordered haddock in the beautiful hotel restaurant while the American told him he was fired, with a month's salary. CACI Europe, he explained, was now to be run by a senior vice president from the States and by Ian Palmer, who had been the first person Tony had recruited to the operation.

'But this is England, Bill,' Tony protested. 'You can't just do things like that over here. I've worked for the company for six years.'

'But I am going to do it,' Fain replied.

'I'll sue,' Tony laughed.

'I'll see you in court,' Fain shrugged.

The reason for the firing was simple, according to Tony. He believes it was because CACI in Europe was only making a 19 per cent gross profit. The 'general and administrative' charges, which American companies levy, had hit his bottom line too hard. Tony claimed he had also been taking the 'long view' on some projects, planning to make bigger profits in the future by taking on less paying projects in the short term.

It is a common syndrome in companies that become successful and where the founders, for whatever reason, decide it is time to start reaping rewards for their past efforts. They begin to resent putting more money in and look for ways to take more out. Within eight years Tony would be seeking to do the same thing himself with JMA, and coming up against colleagues who firmly believed that for the greatest possible harvest the company should continue to invest and plan for the long-term future, even if it meant lower short-term gains. At CACI, however, Tony was still thinking along strategic lines. Those with financial holdings in the company had other ideas.

CACI was in a state of fluctuation at that time, and six months later William Fain himself was also fired.

Tony's firing came like a bolt from the blue and he had to think fast about his next move. He prided himself on being a 'people-oriented' manager. If you are in the consultancy business being 'good with people' is a vital ingredient for success. It was obvious to him that he would have to set up a new company. He was confident that he could do it, but he had to move fast to consolidate his position with all the people he would need to help him, and he had to come up with a new business plan quickly. The adrenalin was pumping, and the ideas began to crowd into his mind. He worked like a whirlwind to keep everyone informed and excited about every project he could dream up, knowing that many of them would not take off quickly enough to succeed, but determined not to lose all the ground which he had gained in the industry during the 1970s.

One of the most important people to his plans was Ian Palmer, who was taking over from him at CACI. Ian is a very different character to Tony. Where Tony is positive, ebullient and often carried away by his own enthusiasms, Ian is cautious, quiet and reflective. If Tony Carter looks like a nightclub bouncer, Ian is more in the mould of Woody Allen. Throughout their working lives together the two of them have acted as opposite forces on one another. Where Tony rushes into new schemes with enthusiasm, Ian slows him down with cautious cross-examination. It hasn't always led to a harmonious personal relationship, but at that stage it provided a solid foundation for a working team. Later, as both men grew more certain that their individualistic approaches to the business were the right ones and that the other one's personality would lead to JMA's downfall, their differences became destructive rather than constructive.

At one stage their feuding and political manoeuvring looked as if it might actually destroy the company that both of them had worked so hard to build up. They virtually had to be held apart by their fellow directors, like two brawlers outside a pub at closing time. In the beginning, however, they were too excited about the future and too busy with the work to waste time worrying about their differences.

Born and brought up in New Zealand, Ian started his working life as a teacher in the maths and science fields, and decided that computing would be a fascinating area to get into in the early 1960s. He still seems more like an eccentric schoolmaster than an entrepreneur, complete with wild hair, thick glasses and rumpled, unco-ordinated wardrobe. One colleague commented that the only things in Ian's wardrobe which matched were his ties.

Deciding that New Zealand was too much of a backwater for a young man with high ambitions, he set out for England in 1969. At the time he was working for ICL, who did not want him to leave them. He made it clear that he would be going whether they backed him or not, and they offered him a job in their London office. He did not find the British ICL operation as suited to his temperament as the New Zealand equivalent, and moved first to Singer to gain computer-user experience and then on to Scicon.

He was already feeling a yearning for a more entrepreneurial situation, where he would have more freedom to develop the ideas which were forming in his mind, and was consequently interested when CACI advertised for venture managers to get projects started in different European cities—the job which Tony was later to take on in London. After a meeting in Munich with William Fain, Ian put himself forward, but finally decided that his background wasn't quite right for the job. When Ian later saw Tony advertising for consultants he made contact again, and William Fain suggested to Tony that Ian would make an ideal working partner.

Ian was already well-known in the database technology industry, which was not an area which CACI was specifically thinking about at the time. Apart from the business which Ian and Tony built up in Europe, the company never really got into database technology—with a few exceptions in the USA.

In 1972, while at Scicon, Ian published the first book on the emerging technology, *Database Management*, which was later reprinted as *Database Systems: A Practical Reference*. The book was immensely successful and established his reputation almost immediately. His ideas broke new ground, establishing him in Europe as a leading figure in the industry. The book started life as a report for his employers, Scicon, which the company decided not to act upon. Ian offered it to QED, an American publisher specializing in computing topics, who turned it into an international bestseller.

In the text Ian predicted that every company would come to have a database, and the book was used as a textbook at establishments like MIT and Harvard. Although database management was then an unproven technology, Ian predicted that it would become the centre of all data processing, and that companies would need the help of consultants for designing their databases.

At the time these ideas were considered revolutionary, although within ten years they were looked upon as obvious. Now virtually every computer is sold with a database capacity before anything else, and every business in the world is becoming aware that they must be able to collect, store and use data correctly if they hope to survive into the future.

When Ian saw Tony's advertisement for people to help him set up a consultancy doing database work he felt this was an opportunity to build something new that was intensely interesting to him. Tony was delighted to have Ian on the team at CACI, since his reputation as a consultant was something tangible to sell to clients from the beginning, when the consultancy had no track record outside America. Tony's entrepreneurial experience and Ian's technical experience fitted together perfectly.

After being fired, therefore, Tony wanted to re-form the partnership in whatever new venture he set up, which meant coaxing Ian away from CACI, along with all the other consultants whom he had recruited, trained and worked alongside over the previous six years.

AN URGE TO CHANGE
THE WORLD

- What will make companies successful in the future?
- What should they be doing about it today?
- As technology races and twists into new forms the attacker has the advantage over the defender.

Companies that do not change will not be able to adapt to the future and will perish, just like the dinosaurs. That is a viewpoint with which most modern management thinkers would agree. Not all of them, however, agree on what shape those changes should take.

Because he spends so much of his time working with models of the future and working to understand the likely effects on businesses and people, James Martin has some very strong ideas on what companies will need to do to survive over the next few decades, and he doesn't hesitate to tell senior managers what he believes.

As corporations become fully electronic, it is vital that senior managers understand the changes which have to take place, whether it is in products, services, fabrication techniques, selling techniques, decision-making, flows of information, mechanisms of control, or management structures.

Although there is a revolution taking place in data processing, many information-systems departments in companies of all sizes are not moving fast enough to the higher-productivity techniques. There is often psychological or political resistance to the new methods, which management needs to overcome. Most people are uncomfortable with change, and will resist it for as long as they possibly can. If they leave it too long it may be too late, but if they set their minds to it they can make continuous change and evolution into a habit.

If they want to survive and prosper in the future, senior managers have to ensure that their organizations are migrating away from slow methods of data processing, and can respond rapidly to information needs by using fourth-generation languages, information-centre techniques, flexible databases, and the maximum automation of the data-processing functions.

Decision-makers at all levels must have the best possible tools for making the best possible decisions, and the necessary information resources have to be made available to them. The way to do this, according to Martin, is to ensure that information engineering has been installed throughout the enterprise. The concept of information engineering was invented by Martin and was endorsed by IBM twelve years later.

To be successful, information engineering requires top–down management of information resources through data modelling and strategic planning networks. In the past these essential aspects of managing a computerized corporation have often failed because of organizational and political factors. Often, Martin believes, they have been managed at too low a level. For changes to be successful, Martin believes, top management must understand the need for them and ensure that an appropriate information infrastructure is built.

Companies must avoid becoming trapped in bureaucracy. They must be ready and willing to change all the time to meet new challenges and to respond to technological developments and market demands. They must also avoid arrogance. Once that starts to creep into any organization it is the beginning of the end because the managers will stop listening to advice and close their ears to new ideas.

Any company that wants to be successful over a long period must have the capability to continually re-invent the world, to change its products and services and ways of working when necessary. Every company should contain champions of change who are strong enough to forge ahead on their own initiative.

This is the mission which JMA was being set up to fulfil for its clients.

PLANNING A NEW CORPORATION

STARTING FROM SCRATCH

- How to build a consultancy from nothing, and finding the best possible partners.

- Never be afraid to associate with the 'greats'. They will make you great by association.

- Find the best people in the world and then go after them. Don't limit yourself to being a big fish in a small pond.

Tony Carter left the Dorchester breakfast meeting with his mind racing. The London rush hour was in full flood, with six lanes of traffic roaring up and down Park Lane as people struggled to get to their offices and first appointments on time. Being fired had come as a complete shock to him and he was trying to marshal his thoughts into some sort of order. It was now a question of limiting the damage to his career and fighting for survival while he was still at the centre of things.

He knew he was going to have to start again, but he couldn't see a clear picture of how he would go about it. He needed time to assimilate what had happened and decide how to handle the situation.

He went back to his home at Fleet in Hampshire and sat down to think out his position. Word soon got out about what had happened and by four o'clock in the afternoon the telephone had started to ring. Everyone connected with the company was stunned, just as they would be again eight years later. They had all been under the impression that they were a happy and successful team. Some could understand the reasoning of the CACI management, but none had foreseen the sacking. Some felt hopeful that without Tony the company would be able to grow even faster, others did not think the sacking was a wise move for the company to take. They all expressed their sympathies and asked what his plans were. It was still too soon for him to say anything, but the ideas were beginning to form.

By Monday morning he had decided that he was definitely going to set up on his own. The company would be in the same business as CACI, but this time he would have an equity stake. He did not intend to be in a position where he could be removed by others again after putting in years of hard work to build something lasting. This time the company would be his, and he would be generous in the equity stakes which he would offer to the people he took on. In the consultancy business you are only as good as your people, and if your people are the best in the business the chances are that they are going to be tempted to go into business on their own, exactly as Tony was planning to do. The only way to keep them is to make sure that they have a big enough stake in the company to make it worth their while staying on, and not taking the risk of going it alone.

The flaw in this argument is that if you find enough good people you will have to give away more than half of the equity in order both to tempt them to join and motivate them to stay. That means that if, for any reason, everyone should gang up against you, you are still vulnerable. Even if your financial stake in the company is safe you can still lose your power and position. Tony did not foresee this at the beginning; he was focusing on building a successful business as fast as possible, he was the prime mover, the undisputed captain of whatever ship he was able to build. The possibility that he might one day be toppled from power seemed remote.

From that moment Tony's prime objective was to get back into business; clearing up his position with CACI was a relatively minor consideration, an irritation which had to be dealt with.

Tony was sure that under his guidance CACI had been working in the right field. There was already a lot of money to be made in database consultancy, and he was certain that the industry was on the verge of something even bigger. Word was spreading through the business community about the power of database management and the opportunities which it offered. He also believed that, by and large, the CACI principles of good management were sound, despite the fact that CACI's growth rate was beginning to slow down. With a few adjustments he felt he could make them work even more successfully in a start-up venture.

Many different elements were coming together in the world of information technology at the beginning of the 1980s. All around the world the pressures of competition were hotting up and it produced a snowballing effect. If one major player in a commercial sector takes onboard some new technology that gives them a competitive advantage, all the others have to follow suit. In competitive situations like that speed would always be of the essence, which meant that the companies have to buy-in the right expertise quickly and the only way to do that is to hire consultants.

In developed countries the increasing rates of deregulation in the business world were forcing the pace of change and improvement even further, and manufacturing industries everywhere were going to come under intense pressures. The snowballing effect of automation within factories was building up a momentum which was unstoppable. At IBM Tony had heard of a stunning 7000 per cent increase in productivity on one production line after a change-over to greater automation had been made. Once companies have tasted a productivity increase like that they become hungry for more, and are far more open to ideas from outside which might help them to do even better.

The speed of change in high-technology everywhere was increasing at a frightening rate. Every intelligently led company wanted to be part of it, but they needed help. They needed guidance through the jungle of hardware, but more especially they needed people to help them cut a path through the mass of software on the market. Every new system that was coming out was offering the earth, and it was impossible for a layperson, however senior, to have any idea which systems were most suited to their needs, or how to implement them so that they became fully integrated parts of the business operation.

Whereas in the past high-technology had merely been used to make current procedures more efficient, the nature of the whole industry was changing. The most aggressive companies, whether they were manufacturing cars, selling soft drinks, financial services or oil, now needed technology to help them make pre-emptive strikes against their competitors. Companies who were aware of what was happening in the world, and who wanted to ensure that they were at the forefront of their industries in ten or twenty years' time, wanted to change the nature of their activities completely, in order to improve efficiency, cost effectiveness, and qualities of manufacture and service.

Although CACI had done well in helping these companies, Tony felt that in the future it should be possible to take the work further into systems development with a team of people like Ian Palmer. If the new company was to take off quickly, however, it needed a big name to front it, someone whose authority in the field was indisputable. Tony and Ian might have been in the business a long time, and they might have a wide range of contacts, but there was no way that their names were known to a wide public. Who, Tony asked himself, was the biggest database guru at the time? The answer was James Martin, who had just published a book called *Information Engineering*, but had been established at the top of the tree for many years before that.

Martin was a partner in a company he co-founded called DMW (Doll Martin World), with a telecommunications expert, Dixon Doll. The two men had met while working at the Systems Research Laboratories of IBM and at the time had a healthy mutual respect for one another.

DMW was a US-based consultancy which they had formed together. Martin had founded another company called Database Design International (DDI), which was later to change its name to Knowledgeware.

Tony had had dealings with DMW while at CACI, because they had wanted him to market their products in Europe. He knew about James Martin's work, and felt sure that the theories and practices which he was promoting were the way the industry was going to go. The question was, would someone like Martin, who was already a multi-millionaire, be interested in going into business with a complete stranger who had nothing to offer but his past experience and his determination to build something worth while? The only way to find out was to go over and ask—and Tony had never been afraid to ask for what he wanted.

On the Monday after he was fired, he called Dixon Doll at his consulting company at Ann Arbor in Michigan, on the outskirts of Detroit, and asked if he would be interested in setting up a company to distribute their products in Europe, offering him 5 per cent of the equity. Tony was doing what he knew best, selling his dreams with enthusiasm, and Dixon was interested. Like most American business people in his position, he was keen to break into the European market, but needed a strong partner to help him achieve it.

American business people are sometimes surprisingly insular. Perhaps it is because the size of the home market makes it unnecessary for most companies to have to venture out into the big bad world in search of new business. When they make attempts to cross the Atlantic, US companies sometimes make the mistake of treating the European market in the same way as the American one. All too often they discover, to their cost, that things happen very differently in the old world. People are motivated by different factors, and organizations operate in different ways. Many American companies have made several attempts on Europe before they either give up and go back to concentrating on the market they know, or stumble on a successful formula which really does work worldwide—like Coca Cola or McDonalds.

During the following week Tony put together a business plan which involved teaming up with all the same people he had worked with at CACI. If he could convince Doll and Martin that he had a strong team behind him, he was more likely to win their confidence. Likewise, if he could talk Doll and Martin into working with him he would have a stronger package to offer to the consultants he was after. At that time, however, he didn't know if CACI would fight to keep their people away from him or not. In the end his own legal battle with his former employers only reached the reconciliation court, where Tony agreed to accept three months' salary, not feeling inclined to expend his energies on fighting a prolonged and expensive legal battle for the sake of a few thousand pounds. He wanted to save his strength and concentrate it in more positive directions. CACI insisted on his signing a contract agreeing not to hire any of their people for six months, but that didn't prohibit him from talking to them. On that first Monday morning, however, he had signed no agreement at all, and was free to meet and talk with all his former colleagues in any way he chose.

He called a meeting for anyone who was interested, to be held at a hotel in London's Drury Lane on the following Sunday. About thirty people turned up, although many of them only wanted to find out what he was planning to do, so that they could protect their own interests. At that stage no one was sure what was going to happen, either at CACI or with Tony's many schemes. None of them had to worry too much about not being able to find other jobs should they need them; it was just a question of deciding which would be the best career moves to make in the circumstances. Everyone was keeping their options open.

CACI had been a typical American company, demanding high performance from everyone, and encouraging a 'hard-sell' approach, something which Tony himself was good at. Many of their management concepts and ideas he assimilated and used for the formation of his new operation. He also believed, however, that he had been acting as something of a buffer between his people in Europe and the American management, taking the knocks on their behalf and allowing them to work and develop at their own pace. He felt that many of them were anxious about what would happen to them now that he was out of the company. Tony did not mince his words. He told them that their protection had now gone, they had, in rugby jargon, lost their 'front row forward'.

He was able to tell them that Bolton House Securities, a venture capital company owned by a friend of his, had agreed to put up £350,000 as setting-up money, and that he had agreement in principle to set up DMW in Europe. He told them that he would be talking to each of them individually about coming over to join him. He believed that he knew which parts of the CACI operation were not turning in profits high enough to satisfy the Americans, and he concentrated on the people running these parts, working at winning their confidence. He knew that they would soon be in the employment marketplace, and he wanted them to know that he would welcome them into his new company.

Tony was particularly keen to take Ian Palmer with him, in order to recreate their successful partnership. Ian was initially happy to stay at CACI and see what happened, being unsure what he wanted to do with his career next. His brief from America now that Tony had gone was to make the company more profitable, which he didn't find hard to do. Ian cut one project which was unprofitable, concentrated the company's efforts, reduced wastage, increased utilization and raised the rates.

Within six months he too realized that his time at CACI was limited. He could see that changes in CACI in the States were likely to result in plans which did not include him. From outside Tony was bombarding him with plans, ideas and promises, none of which yet seemed to be founded on anything solid. Ian continued to wait and see what would develop.

THE ODD COUPLE

TEAMING UP WITH THE BEST

- A great guru or teacher must spend more time learning than teaching.
- If a guru is claiming to be able to predict the future, he must have a track record for accuracy.
- The people with the ideas must be able to work with the people who know how to turn those ideas into reality.
- Without good communication nothing will happen.

At that stage Tony had only met James Martin in passing, and by 1983 Martin was already established as a powerful world figure. His success was becoming the stuff of legend and to gain time with him was hard. He was due to give a seminar at Ann Arbor, Dixon Doll's home town and the seat of the local university and high-technology industries, so Tony set out there to meet the two men together, and to put forward his proposition in more detail.

Jim Martin remembers meeting Tony for the first time at a cocktail party in Ann Arbor. Tony seemed to him to be a people-orientated, hard-drinking, mover-and-shaker, likely to take the sort of risks which Dixon Doll would never dare to attempt. As with the relationship between Tony and Ian, Tony and Jim were also precise opposites. While Tony was an avid rugby player, Jim prided himself on taking no exercise at all.

While Jim was a 'thinker', Tony was a 'doer'. Tony also knew the European market intimately, which neither Jim nor Dixon did. There seemed to be no overlap in their areas of expertise.

At that time Tony saw the collaboration with DMW and DDI as opportunities to capitalize on Jim's name and reputation and to gain access to products which could be marketed and sold on an agency basis. On the back of these activities he could build the consultancy and teaching practice in Europe. While quite comfortable with this concept, Jim was already hatching ideas about how a consultancy with a strong methodology could automate their services and change the whole ball game.

Although he is one of the most respected of industry figures, Jim has never been, nor wanted to be, a business executive tied to a desk. He has interests in so many diverse operations that he has little time or taste for deskbound management. When it becomes necessary he is quite capable of taking over the reins from most of his senior executives, but he prefers to let them get on with running their businesses, as long as they are performing up to expectations, and leave himself free for the things that he enjoys.

All his greatest business achievements have been done in tandem with someone else running the show. Jim is more interested in ideas, how they work and what they will mean. He understands the business process very well, particularly when applied to huge, multinational corporations. He is a strategic thinker with a proven track record, but that doesn't mean that he wants to run a business himself on a day-to-day basis. He finds being a loner more fun and more lucrative. Tony, however, is first and foremost an entrepreneur and motivator of people. The two of them went well together.

Jim sees his role as looking at all the new trends in computing, putting them into perspective, sorting them out, clarifying them and then explaining them tutorially. Whereas other writers on the subject are aiming at academic distinction—which is often sought through the use of complicated and obscure language—Jim always seeks to put across complicated ideas with simplicity and clarity. On stage he is an electrifying communicator and performer; off-stage he is a tall, preoccupied, professorial figure. He is curiously shy. At present unmarried, he claims he has difficulty meeting women because of his shyness. He dresses and grooms himself like the powerful businessmen he is used to advising. He looks like one of them, but it seems to be like a costume for a part he is playing, a way of gaining their confidence and their respect, so that they will pay attention and give weight to the ideas which he is putting before them. If he looked like a university professor they might perhaps dismiss him. As it is he looks and talks like their equal. He is as successful as them, and usually a great deal wealthier, having made fortunes in several different areas, and therefore worthy of their time.

In order to remain the most successful operator in his business, he has to continue learning all the time. The most successful guru is the fastest learner. One of the best ways to learn is to consult, since the very nature of the work means that you become privy to the problems that are besetting the market, and have to apply solutions. The more widely the net can be cast around the world in search of problems and solutions, the more detailed and far-reaching the guru's knowledge will become.

Jim's predictions throughout the 1970s and '80s have proved to be remarkably close to the mark, and they have established a reputation for him as a seer. He has been right so many times in the past, people feel obliged to take everything he says seriously. When a big company in the technology market misses a major future trend it risks missing out on billions of pounds worth of market share. If talking to Jim Martin for a couple of days might help them to avoid that danger, then they will be happy to pay whatever fee he asks. If, while talking to them, Jim sees that what they need is an ongoing consultancy service to build a methodology which will actually work, then he needs to be able to pass them on to others with more detailed, specialist knowledge. Tony intended to provide a team which could fulfil that role, first in Europe, then in America and the rest of the world.

Jim predicted the growth of teleprocessing, of on-line storage and real-time systems. He forecasted markets in microcomputers, database systems, computer networks, satellites, optical fibres and hobby computing. He pioneered the growth of information engineering and CASE tools (Computer-Aided Software Engineering).

These successes have meant that he has been able to attract increasingly large audiences for his seminars, and to charge more than the average daily rate for attendance. Most of his seminars draw 200 or so people at between $2,000 and $3,000 a head (making a total of around $500,000 each time).

He saw his role in Tony's plan as being the provider of ideas and thoughts, which Tony and his consultants could spread around the business world and turn into real applications. Jim would provide the guidelines and philosophies which the consultancy would be founded on, and would keep throwing ideas at it. If there was some particularly interesting piece of consultancy work offered, which would add to his sum total of understanding, then he would handle it himself. On the whole, however, he would continue with his personal business, and leave Tony to run his.

The resulting company has come remarkably close to that first vision, but not without some terrifyingly close calls on the way. Jim continued to throw ideas at Tony, and found him to be receptive and open to them. He believes that about a third of what he suggested actually came to fruition. He gave Tony things which he could sell, and showed him what was possible. Tony told him what was happening in the business, what was succeeding and what was failing, and Jim would counsel him on what the likely outcome of certain moves would be. As long as the business was growing and on course, the relationship worked perfectly.

Jim was born at the end of the 1930s in Ashby de la Zouche, a market town in northern England, 16 miles outside Leicester. From this basic coal-mining area and 'a very ordinary family', Jim made it to the dreaming spires of Oxford University, where he received both a bachelor's and a master's degree in physics and a strong ambition to enjoy the good things in life. He later gained an honorary doctorate of science and still claims to see things from a physics point of view.

After a two-year stint as an army officer, he applied for more than a dozen jobs before joining IBM UK. These days, when IBM is one of the most powerful and wealthy companies in the world, it is hard to remember that at the end of the 1950s and beginning of the 1960s the computing industry was still in its infancy, and IBM was nowhere close to becoming the world force it is today. A bright young man could rise fast in this fledgling industry. In 1961 Jim was sent to America as a trainee and, later, went back to work as a programmer on the American Airlines SABRE project, which was the world's first commercial teleprocessing system. He also coded assembler language on a follow-up project for Pan American World Airways.

The SABRE system was the first to use terminals connected by telecommunications to a central computer for making bookings and storing details about passengers.

A decade later American Airlines were looking for a way to harness the growing trend for ticket booking through travel agencies. They believed that in the future most of their business would come via this route, and they wanted to find a way of capitalizing on this source of income. They needed a new version of SABRE, which involved putting computer terminals into travel agencies across America, giving them an ability to check availability and make bookings within seconds. The system also carried information on competing airlines, but American Airlines, having taken the initiative, was able to guide the purchasers towards their products. It was a quantam leap for the airline industry and for the teleprocessing business. It required great courage on the part of American Airlines' management, but it increased the airline's share of the market by 20 per cent at a time when many of their competitors were going bankrupt. The SABRE System was capable of processing well over a thousand transactions per second, pushing back the frontiers of technology and completely altering the way 'things are done' in the airline booking industry.

It was an example of using new technology to make pre-emptive strikes against the competition, rather than just automating what was already there.

It was this sort of strategic thinking which was beginning to mark out the companies that would do well in the coming years. It took courage on the part of the management to undertake such major changes, which could alter the entire working and management structures of a company overnight. Installing a system of this sort is a major business risk, and the decisions have to be taken at the very top of the company. The decision-makers sitting on the boards of giant companies are not computer experts and they need advice from people they can trust.

Top management at General Motors has stated: 'new technology must be integrated with new social systems to form new human partnerships. This requires new types of plant and new types of management.' It means that the changeover to new systems will never be comfortable. It will make many people feel threatened and apprehensive, uncertain what the future holds in store for them. There are many companies who wait too long to pluck up the courage to make the jump, and lose valuable market share as a result. The problem is that it is possible to continue without changing and adapting. A company which is not doing well can continue to survive for years, even decades, by retrenching and contracting. Old habits can be maintained and still enough business will come in to keep the company afloat. Before long, however, they have grown too small to be able to afford to invest in the equipment and systems which they should have been moving on to in the beginning. Soon they become second- and third-rate powers in their own industries and eventually they are doomed to extinction, having missed out on the evolutionary cycle just like the dinosaurs before them.

To get this message across, the computer industry desperately needs good communicators, who can make themselves understood by senior executives and can put across the right messages to the right people.

Despite the fact that he had come from the technical side of the business, Jim proved early that he could communicate well. After a two-year stay in Paris, at IBM's world trade office, he won IBM World Trade's biggest sales order to date — a world-wide reservation system for BOAC, part of the company now known as British Airways. The system became known as BOADICEA.

Although Jim was a systems engineer and not a salesman IBM asked him to handle the account when the previous salesman proved unable to sell them anything. The salesman who was removed from the account was called John Hoskyns, later to become Sir John and head of the Institute of Directors, who later went on to form his own consultancy and advise Mrs Thatcher. There is, however, only a very thin line between being a good 'communicator' and a good 'salesman'. As his career developed, Jim was able to walk this line very deftly.

The airlines were at that time on the leading edge of technology, and Jim was right at the forefront of where the most innovative work was being done. It gave him an unusual perspective into the way society was likely to change and develop as technology moved on into other areas. If teleprocessing had worked so well for an airline, why wouldn't it work for a bank, or a retailer or a car-hire business? In fact there was hardly a business on earth which did not need information in order to sell itself and its products more effectively. If they needed information, then they needed systems to manage it effectively.

He was approached by the business publishers Prentice-Hall Inc. to write his first book when he was just 25 years old. It was called *Programming Real Time Computer Systems*, and was published in 1963. This was the first inkling that Jim had of what he might be able to do in the world outside IBM.

Since then he has gone on to become the world's highest selling author of computer books—around seventy titles so far—and has made over 300 video and computer-based training course modules with Applied Learning International in Naperville.

To start with, however, he remained within IBM at the same time as writing the books. From Paris he was called back to America and offered a position in the company's New York-based Systems Research Institute, where he began to create a serious reputation. He had already had twelve books published by then and was a popular lecturer, using innovative teaching techniques such as multiple screens and sound tracks.

Being at the heart of IBM at this crucial time in the company's development gave Jim access to a very powerful research capability. He made full use of all the information that came his way to formulate his predictions about how the industry would go. It was the accuracy of these predictions which began to catch the attention of a wider audience, particularly in the world of big business.

IBM, however, was too procedure-orientated to be comfortable with this maverick in their midst. The company's philosophies did not allow for members of staff to become superstars. With the onset of anti-trust action against the company, the IBM lawyers began to censor his books. It sometimes took them longer to check the books than it had taken Jim to write them. He decided that the time had come for him to become an 'industry spokesman' rather than an 'IBM spokesman'.

In 1977 he took a year's sabbatical in order to travel and initiate his world seminars in telecommunications, database management, teleprocessing and distributed data processing. He was surprised by just how much money he could command for his performances, considerably more than the president of IBM was making in salary, and he decided to stay on the outside for good. He later told *Business Magazine* that he wished he had done it ten years earlier. 'Most people are trapped in organizations,' he said, 'thinking they need the comfort of a large structure. Most can get more interest and more money by themselves.'

The money-making machine began to pick up speed. His Prentice-Hall royalties grew to more than $1 million a year after taxes. Besides the high fees which he charges for his seminars, he also gets a percentage of the gate, and then he has his personal stakes in fast-growing companies like JMA and KnowledgeWare.

As well as consulting with the top management of the large computer industry organizations about their corporate product strategies, he advises many organizations on their implementation of new DP methods. He has been a high-level adviser to several governments, and was a member of the first joint American–Russian committee to study possible exchanges of computer expertise.

As with anyone in such a visible position, Jim has his opponents. There are those in the industry who believe that he is simply a zealot who has the knack of communicating with top management. No one, however, can say that he isn't a powerful figure within the industry, and most people believe that his early books were the most important to be written in their area. It is possible that in a few years' time his current books on information engineering and rapid application development will be seen as even more important. Some people complain that his ideas are too way out, but the same critics have mostly not seen the way in which JMA consultants have been able to make Jim's theories work at a nuts-and-bolts level. No one doubts that Martin has done a matchless job of alerting top management to the need for technology and in making them excited about the possibilities.

By the time Tony Carter arrived in Ann Arbor, Jim was already a multi-millionaire with a famous house in Bermuda boasting its own private beach with a natural arch blasted out of the rocks by the waves.

Jim always seems most at home in the relaxed settings of his homes. His workrooms have windows with wide, peaceful horizons. In Bermuda he looks out over the ocean, in Vermont he overlooks ski resorts and mountains, and in New Zealand he gazes at gentle green, sheep-speckled hills. All the rooms are different. In some you find nothing but James Martin books in thirty different languages, in others you find oriental art and grand pianos which visitors often believe Jim is playing — only to discover that it is a computer on-line to the piano. All Jim's electronic equipment may look like the toys of a rich man, but they are all fuel for Jim's wider vision of how the world will be in the future.

Martin's homes offer the perfect atmosphere for a modern thinker and philosopher. To contrast with the computers in the house, there are the wide open, wild spaces outside. Jim is more at home walking in the mountains and taking visitors down to rough and ready local inns for beer, hamburgers and chips, than he is at formal city dinner parties with corporation heads.

Many of the most powerful business people in the world have taken their jets and helicopters out to the houses to spend days with Jim, sharing his casual lifestyle, and searching for ideas on where the global marketplace is going. Not only has he written about technology, he has also created markets for it by talking about products and ideas at the seminars, writing about them in books and discussing them on videos. More than any other individual, Jim has created a market for Computer Aided Software Engineering (CASE) technology (CASE means, in layman's terms, creating software programs which are capable of writing other software far faster and better than any human programmers), simply by spreading the word at the highest levels. Some of the most far-reaching decisions in the international software scene have probably been inspired by conversations held on those rough wooden benches in barn-like dives called Mooselips and The Common Man.

Many of the most successful products in the market were created by Jim and a number of whizz-kid hackers from his various associated companies, as they worked late into the night at the houses, breaking new barriers and moving the industry forward in quantum leaps.

When guests from the business world come to stay with Jim there are no battalions of servants to wait on them, everything is 'help yourself' and get back to work. It is back to the world of the American pioneers, working to push across new boundaries rather than revelling in the rewards of past successes.

When a man is selling his time at the same prices as ex-prime ministers of European countries and ex-secretaries of state in America, he doesn't want to waste any of it on tiresome administrative tasks. Jim hates anything to do with administration. Not being comfortable within the confines of a large organization, he now needs people to help with the handling of the organizational and financial aspects of his success. He uses his time to think, read, talk, play with computers, write and teach as much as possible. In order to do that he needs to have other people look after the business. Just like a star from the world of entertainment, he needs people to organize his personal appearances, publish his books and sell his consulting time and ideas. It was in the latter area that Tony Carter suggested a mutually beneficial relationship.

Also at the meeting in Ann Arbor was Don Brown, the president of Jim's company Database Design Inc (DDI—later called KnowledgeWare), with whom Tony was later to clash swords violently. Over four days of meetings Tony put forward his business plan, which both Dixon and Jim liked. On the last day they had lunch and went into the final negotiating stage; Dixon always liked to hold meetings in other people's homes and that day they were at his secretary's house. Jim suggested that they should forget about the venture capital and finance the company themselves, splitting the equity three ways.

At that stage Jim did not have interests in many companies, only DDI (KnowledgeWare) and a minority share of DMW. He was just emerging as a man with the potential to put venture capital into enterprises which caught his eye. He was often willing to back ideas which he liked, and he was always completely loyal to the people who helped him along the way, even when it might have been in his best interests financially to sever relationships.

One of the points which Tony later tried to put across to Jim, never completely successfully, was that rather than betting simply on ideas he should be betting on people. Whenever Jim has had a major business success it has been because he was associated with good business people who knew how to run companies. Higher Order Software, for instance, was an idea for developing real-time systems which was technically wonderful, but which had disastrous management, whereas Intech who sold a product called Excelerator were a well run company, and Jim consequently reaped massive rewards.

Martin's initial reaction to Tony Carter was one of extreme caution, a bit like a nineteenth-century native meeting an English missionary. The two of them could hardly have been more different. Martin, the elegantly dressed, anti-athletic, lanky aesthete, living in a world of ideas and machines; Carter, the muscular rugby player, fired from his job at CACI and seeking to 'press the flesh' of someone who could help him to make money. They made an odd couple.

To Tony, Jim Martin seemed too gentle to be capable of giving him the same sort of trouble that William Fain had given him. He didn't believe Jim would ever be able to fire him and he saw the potential of the odd couple working together, complementing each other. Tony believed that Jim looked on him as a person who would be able to help him make money in a partnership. They were so different that they would be able to stay out of one another's hair. At the same time Martin saw a swashbuckling figure, rough and tough, and capable of building and leading a company based on new ideas.

It was the start of an enigmatic and warm relationship that was sometimes comic and always colourful, a marriage of opposites. They grew to respect and trust one another.

Some years later a delegate at one of Martin's seminars, who had seen the odd couple together on a number of occasions, was heard to remark that 'James Martin has the best-dressed bodyguard you could imagine.'

Carter was not as rich as either Martin or Doll. Determined to be an equal partner he suggested that they each put up $68,000—which was the most he felt they needed to find—and that the rest should be raised on a bank loan from the Bank of Bermuda, personally guaranteed by the three of them. Because of his home in Bermuda, Jim was well known to the bank, and there seemed to Tony to be considerable advantages at the time to banking off-shore. To protect each other Martin and Carter signed an agreement freezing their ownership of JMA into a fixed ratio. This would prevent either from scheming financially against the other. The agreement led to a strife-free relationship but unfortunately prevented Martin investing more money in JMA when it badly needed it later on.

The holding company for DMW, which wholly owned Tony's new European company, was also set up in Bermuda. It was by then only the end of June, less than two months after the fateful meeting at the Dorchester in London, and it was likely to be some months before they would need to call upon the bank for the money.

The first brick in the new company was now firmly in place, but in the background there were still the rumblings from the past. Tony's settlement from CACI, which would give him the necessary money for his stake in DMW, was still being argued over, and there were plans and structures to be worked out. At the same time Tony and Pat were trying to resolve their marital problems.

Pat travelled to Ann Arbor with Tony, and once the meetings were over the two of them went on to their house on Amelia Island in Florida, to spend July relaxing, and trying to work out where they should go from there. Years later, after Tony was divorced from Pat and his relationship with JMA was very different, the company's executives would still be meeting on Amelia Island, plotting the future together. But at this stage the company was still just a figment of his imagination and Tony was girding his loins for the battles ahead. As well as playing golf, he was also working at his personal fitness, which allowed him at the time to play in the same first fifteen rugby team as his 18-year-old son Simon.

MISSION CRITICAL

MINING FOR INFORMATION

- How can information be more effectively co-ordinated and exploited?

- Information is a natural resource. If it is not exploited imaginatively it simply goes to waste.

- The ability to co-ordinate information systems effectively gives companies the ability to multiply their potential profitability many times over.

- Rather than just being an asset to a company, a brilliant information system can become an integral part of the company's product or service — making it 'mission critical'.

- The vision of just how much is possible must come from the top and be communicated to everyone.

As Jim Martin explains it, there have been four major eras in the coming of computers to business. The First Era was the arrival of punched cards and batch processing. The Second Era saw the installation of terminals, disk storage, teleprocessing and on-line systems. The Third Era involved the evolution of computer networks and information systems which helped with the handling of large amounts of data, bringing spreadsheets and decision support systems. The Fourth Era found the computer becoming the control mechanism of business and providing corporations with competitive weapons which he calls, with a typical sense of the dramatic, 'mission critical' systems.

One of the most important aspects of computing is getting the right information to the right people at the right time. Simply compiling masses of data is not enough. Unless you know how to handle it and what to do with the results, it will lie in unused mountains, taking up the time of the compilers and masking the valuable with the worthless. In order to make it useful the vital pieces of data have to be mined out, like nuggets of gold from miles of useless rock. In order to do that you have to sink mineshafts, networks of tunnels and linking passages, and you have to know what you are looking for. You also need to know how to shape the raw material—information—so that it is saleable and useful.

Unless you know what it is you need the information for, bringing it to the surface will be no more than an interesting exercise, wasting more time and energy. There must be a long-term strategy in place before a company actually sets out in search of the raw materials which it needs to make it competitive.

Information is increasingly being regarded as a strategic resource, not merely a resource for routine data processing. Strategic uses of information are greatly affecting the profits of corporations and will increasingly become keys to corporate survival. The right decisions can only be made if the right information is fed into the process at the beginning. The more relevant information there is, the more likely that the decision will be the best one possible. At certain stages, however, the human brain ceases to be able to take on board any more information, and decisions have to be taken prematurely, with a greater likelihood of failure.

Computers have no such limitations, but they do need systems to ensure that they are looking at the right information, and understanding the precise needs of the business concerned, something which the human brain will know instinctively.

To return to the mining analogy, man could only just scratch the surface of the earth as long as he was relying on his own muscle and a pick and shovel. Once he had managed to automate the process, however, he was able to dive down and discover minerals that he had never dreamed of before. A company might think that it is mining for tin, and discover that it is actually sitting on massive deposits of oil.

Suddenly the whole concept of the company's future has changed. It is worth far more than it was worth the day before, and has the scope to go out searching for oil in a hundred other places. The discovery of oil is useless, however, unless a human brain has first worked out that the sticky black liquid can be used to power engines, and that engines can give the human race heat, light and mobility.

In just the same way, computers open up the possibilities for discovering new ways in which to use information to achieve results, but only human brains can apply it to the real world.

A successful corporate information strategy requires sufficient vision from top management to identify the opportunities that can be achieved through the more effective use of information. Management, in other words, requires a clear vision of where the company is going and how it's going to get there. How can information be used to gain competitive advantage? How can it support key decision-makers? How can it integrate all the functions of the organization with external customers and suppliers?

Effective co-ordination of systems is the only way that wastage of time, money and effort can be eliminated from any operation. The larger the corporation the more likely that efforts are being duplicated and that necessary changes are taking longer to filter through to top management. Consequently the potential gains from creating effective database management systems become greater. The larger the company, however, the more complex the information needed, and the more multi-layered the problems which need solving.

In the near future all competitive companies will be run with a vast mesh of interacting computers and database systems. Computers in one corporation will interact on-line with computers in other corporations—as well as with their customers, suppliers, distributors and anyone else involved in the process of doing business.

Some companies succeed impressively during this latest technological era, gaining direct advantages over their competitors with the use of strategic systems. Some of them are on-line systems which directly enable the corporation to accomplish a mission which wouldn't otherwise be possible—making them mission critical. With the new systems it is possible to take a quantum leap, leaving the competition behind.

The SABRE project which Jim worked on for American Airlines was mission critical because it entirely changed the way that the airline booking business was run.

A mission critical system operates at the heart of a business, performing vital corporate and intercorporate functions. If the system stops, so do those aspects of the business. Although computer systems started life as back-room, paperwork-processing operations—and many still are—they can now actually become the driving force of a corporation, if conceived, designed and built correctly.

Strategic systems can be used to link corporations to their customers, agents, distributors, retailers and suppliers, as well as to software in customer locations, new products, automated fabrication, service innovations, strategic alliances...and so the list goes on.

In order to take the first step, however, the top managers must be able to see ways in which information systems can enhance their competitive position. It requires a sense of vision, and an acceptance of what is new and difficult to understand. Managers who are frightened to take a step into the dark will hesitate too long before taking the plunge, and may be forced into doing it as a defensive measure by more courageous competitors.

In many cases managers are still tied up in the first three eras of technology, and they are more able to see the problems which they have with their existing systems than the opportunities offered by future developments. The thought of investing yet more money on new equipment and consultancy services may be anathema to any company which is not happy with the systems it already has. If the old systems don't work well, why spend money on new ones which might be equally ineffective? The answer is that companies who want to survive have no choice.

Often senior managers complain that they are unable to obtain applications from their company computers when they want them. Sometimes the delays can even stretch into years. It is often difficult, or even impossible, to obtain changes that they need in a reasonable amount of time, simply because the systems are ineffective and outdated, and were not conceived and designed as integrated parts of the corporate process.

A certain amount of the problem has been caused by the hardware and software salespeople of the past eras who had to oversell the products in order to persuade people to buy. Cautious customers have then bought bits and pieces at different times, simply to provide tactical answers to short-term problems, without any long-term plan. The result is that the pieces do not fit together well. Many companies have also not spent enough on hiring and training the best people to get the required results from the equipment, or have been quite content with the initial 'problem-solving' which their system does for them, without looking at the potential which it has to do far more.

Some programmes have errors in them or do not work, and systems delivered often do not match up to the true user requirements. It is often difficult for customers to understand data processing and communicate precise requirements to suppliers of equipment or software. Specifications, on which users have to sign off, are difficult to check and usually full of inconsistencies, omissions and errors. Critics find that systems cost much more to develop and maintain than is ever anticipated. Because of the long time required to obtain results, the most important decision-support systems are never implemented. The support is often needed more quickly than the time needed to create the programmes.

Despite all these problems, most successful business people know that they would be likely to make better decisions with computer assistance. Most management decisions require information. Sometimes the difference between a good or bad decision can cost a company millions of pounds. It might be a decision regarding the transfer of funds among world currencies, or the purchase of a massively used chemical. Whatever the question is, it requires information, comparisons and calculations to find the best possible answer. It also requires an instant response. Questions like these can't wait to be answered while an applications backlog is cleared up, and if they do then opportunities are missed.

It is only in the most sophisticated and enlightened companies, therefore, that the idea of strategic systems has been able to take root. Rigorous business-planning methodologies are needed, with a detailed analysis of goals and the problems to be overcome. Managements must be able to anticipate the impact which the technology will have on their businesses. They must also analyse the critical success factors. Although it is usually the corporate giants who have the funds available for these sorts of exercises, it is often the younger, hungrier companies, which use strategic systems to gain a position in the marketplace, taking business from their more established, but slower moving, competitors.

More than anything else, however, senior managers must have the vision which shows them how technology can change or radically transform their companies, to make them more competitive. That means that the impetus for change must come from the top, even if the ideas are initially triggered by people half-way down the management ladder. The top people must understand the implications, and they must be 100 per cent behind the work which will go into installing the systems.

Strategic systems often require companies to do things in radically different ways, and there is nearly always some resistance to change in any organization. It will only work if the people at the top insist that it does. It is no good simply automating today's corporate functions if those functions are not effective enough. If the company is truly thinking strategically they should be looking for ways to change the corporate functions or build new activities into the corporation. Strategic systems are also major business risks, and those sorts of decisions have to be taken at the top.

Whereas the earlier eras of computing were largely defensive, with companies having to install systems simply to keep up in the race towards greater efficiency and higher productivity, strategic systems are often designed for competitive attack. They provide a way for a corporation to differentiate its services or products from those of its competition.

One of the ways in which change takes place is in the use of personal computers. Most companies buy them, but not many think about their use in strategic terms. To begin with they are seen simply as methods of automating existing tasks. The use of computerized tools and information can encourage better decision-making, and can encourage users to invent better administration procedures and to cut costs. They can increase knowledge about worker productivity, and bypass the development backlog of the information service department.

This task automation phase may well provide a 10 or 20 per cent return on investment, which a company could be very happy with. If, however, a strategic view is taken, using technology to restructure the business processes rather than simply automating them, a return of anything up to 1000 per cent on investment might be possible.

Jim Martin believes there are seven primary objectives of an information strategy:

1. analysing how to gain competitive advantage using new technology;

2. using information as a strategic weapon to attack the competition, to lock in customers but lock out the opposition;

3. tieing the strategy directly to critical success factors identified for the organization;

4. improving decision-making by getting the right information to key decision-makers equipped with the most powerful tools;

5. implementing intercorporate networks that link manufacturers to suppliers, customers, distributors, retailers, financial organizations etc.;

6. creating entirely new businesses or major new thrusts in the operation of current businesses, using strategic information systems;

7. implementing strategic systems rapidly by making the most powerful use of automated tools.

This is the message which he is preaching to the heads of governments and giant corporations, and these systems are what Tony's people were setting out to supply via consultancy and training services.

7

EARLY DAYS

GENERATING INCOMINGS BEFORE OUTGOINGS

- How to win the business before hiring the staff. Choosing the right moments to expand and invest. How to recruit for high-speed growth.

- To start a business with little capital means attending to the question of cashflow from Day One.

- That means getting the work first and then hiring the resources to handle it. But how can you convince a potential client you can do the job without an existing team?

- Successful executives will be brave enough to hire people far better than themselves.

- Recruitment traplines save money and build strong teams.

No matter how famous Martin was, and no matter how sound his ideas, the European business was going to have to survive on its own merits. Customers were going to have to be persuaded that the people Tony Carter was able to gather together could make a difference to their businesses. They had to believe that what Jim Martin was preaching wasn't just a pipe-dream for someone else to follow up, but an attainable goal, something which they could be doing today if they only knew how, and which would make a difference to their bottom line. That meant Tony needed a credible team of people, and a credible message.

In the consultancy business there are two vital ingredients—consultants and clients. In order to get clients you have to have the consultants to service them. In order to pay the consultants you have to get the contracts. It is a 'chicken-and-egg' situation, requiring careful balancing.

When a consultancy is up and running it can afford to take on good people in anticipation of the revenue they will generate in the future. When you are just starting out—and your own money is at stake—you have to try to find the people who will be willing to join you if, or when, you win the business. The answer might be 'contingency recruitment'.

A contingency offer is an offer of employment which has been agreed with a prospective employee in every detail except starting date and first project.

It is the most effective way for a start-up consultancy to overcome the chicken-and-egg situation (which comes first, the order or the consultant?). It also means that the employee is being billed out from day one. It eliminates agency fees and ensures target growth. It allows the consultancy to win orders which would be lost if the right people couldn't be recruited at the right times.

Say, for instance, consultancy managers working on projects were asked by the company's contact within the organization if the consultancy would be interested in quoting for a major database development. The managers are able to persuade the client not to go out to open tender but to use their firm. The contact (these contacts are known as *inside salespeople*), however, cannot be sure when the project would start or whether it would get budget authorization.

The managers convince the inside salesperson that there should be an early start but there are still doubts about the budget. None of the managers' existing project team would be free to work on this new project, so the managers are going to have to recruit.

What would have happened if the managers had waited until the order was confirmed before starting the recruiting process? The chances are that good people would not have been found in time, resulting in an inferior job for the client, or else the starting date would be delayed while waiting for the right people to become available.

If managers recruited before the order, what would happen to their bottom lines if the orders then didn't materialize, or were delayed six months? They would either have to keep paying the new recruits, be prepared to take a loss, and pray that another job will come along quickly, or else they would have to fire the new recruits whom they worked so hard to win. The result of the latter course of action would be some very unhappy ex-employees, who would be going out into the marketplace with very justifiable complaints about the company, which they would undoubtedly share with everyone they met.

The only solution would be to make contingency offers to the right people and hope that the job materialized quickly enough for them not to grow tired of waiting.

The first people who needed to be found at JMA were the project managers, who were the first to start work on any project, and who were usually on one month's notice from their previous employers. A project manager who accepted an offer in the first week or two could then be involved in the recruitment of the team.

The contingency offer has to be sold to prospects positively: 'We want your career to begin on a positive note—we don't want you to join when there is nothing to do. We want to prepare for your arrival. We want you to join when we can devote some time to helping you—this will not be the case for a couple of months.'

The manager doing the recruiting needs to be quite open and honest about the project in hand, perhaps explaining that the only dragon to be slain is board approval, but that might take a few weeks to come through, and so forth.

Once project managers have accepted contingency offers, the consultancy managers then have to keep them on the hook until the order is firmed-up. This means planned contact with them until they are safely on-board. On average it is possible to keep people waiting up to twelve weeks before they lose interest. Contact needs to be frequent at the beginning, dying down a little in the middle and then building up again between the eight- and twelve-week marks.

There are a number of different ways of setting up a consultancy from scratch. One way is to spend a large amount of capital on hiring people and offices, and then go out looking for work for them to do, which means spending more money on marketing. On that basis it is relatively easy to write a strategic business plan, which is different from planning a strategic business.

The sort of business plan which Tony was looking for from his managers when they were setting up in a new centre was more specific. It had to name the names of real potential customers and recruits who were known to the manager and who were likely to be interested in the project. It had to show specifically where the cashflow was going to be coming from. It couldn't be full of ideas on how to hire other people, such as advertising agencies and recruitment consultancies, to do the work. Any money spent on these sorts of services was money off the bottom line, and it was not a style of management which appealed to Tony.

His business plan, which he showed to Jim and the other people he wanted to 'sell' his ideas to, said that he was only planning to lose £50,000 in the first year. That meant he couldn't waste money by building up a payroll of people who wouldn't be earning fees for a few weeks, or even months. Once you have the people lined up, you then have to win the business, using their reputations to demonstrate why the client should use your company. If the contracts take too long to win, however, the people you were hoping to recruit may have lost interest. It is a juggling act, but one which Tony Carter relished.

His agreement with CACI stated that he would not poach anybody for six months. His first recruit from his ex-employer was Eric Magnuson, and Tony had to wait until that six months was up before Eric could actually join him.

Eric was an ideal addition to a team with hopes of becoming international. He is an American who was born and brought up in Europe, making him fluent in French and proficient in a couple of other European languages.

Tony's second recruit was Ian Macdonald. Both these men were still with JMA eight years later. Ian Macdonald had come to CACI from jobs in ICL and Univac, where he had started out as a trainer, a role he was to come back to a few years later once JMA was large enough to set up its own training department. For the first three months they worked on preparing course material using Jim Martin's books as source material. Ian was used to being thrown in at the deep end by Tony, having been one of the earliest recruits to CACI, where he was expected to go out and win new business on his own virtually on his first day. Although he was not a natural entrepreneur, he enjoyed the excitement of the pioneering days in both companies, and had faith that Tony would be able to pull them through to a more secure footing.

Ian's first job was in Wellington, New Zealand, for a client called Databank Systems. Databank provided the computing and communications for all the banks in New Zealand. It was a client which Ian Palmer had picked up during his six months of freelancing between CACI and JMA. He brought the account to JMA. Ian Macdonald was due to get married at the time and managed to take his new bride down with him, stopping off for an exotic honeymoon in Fiji before spending three months in Wellington, among the scenic beauties of New Zealand, and coming back via Hawaii. It was an exciting start.

CACI kept back £5,000 of Tony's settlement until March, and then declined to pay it. Tony half-heartedly threatened to sue them, but not until everyone who could have given evidence against him had joined his new company. In the end he decided that it was not worth pursuing, and put the past completely behind him.

Four days after New Year Ian Palmer rang to tell Tony that he was leaving CACI. He too was tied by a six-month contract, and had not yet decided whether to join up with Tony and start building another company, or whether to take a job as an MIS director in an established company. He decided to work as a freelancer while he considered what to do. He had a number of contracts with companies such as the South Wales Electricity Board to keep him occupied.

Tony was determined to convince Ian to join, and did not let up the pressure, offering him a shareholding, and spelling out all his plans for the future. Ian was finally convinced when Tony started talking about his partnership with Jim Martin, and was able to introduce Ian and Jim at London Airport, where the two gurus had a three-hour meeting which demonstrated to both that they were thinking along the same lines. Jim had read Ian's book some years before, and was well aware of his status in the industry. By putting them together Tony was able to kill two birds with one stone, impressing both sides at once with his ability to attract top people in the industry to work with him. Ian joined him as technical director in July, bringing his existing clients with him.

The setting up of DMW in Europe, as JMA was first called, involved Tony in four separate jobs. First was the recruitment, second was the selling, third was the general administration and strategic planning for the company and fourth was actually consulting and teaching. It is a problem which most entrepreneurs face, if they are setting up without a massive amount of money behind them. The most difficult decision is usually how best to allocate their time. Should they try to split themselves between so many different roles, risking doing all of them badly? Or should they hire expensive managers to take over parts of the operation—and if so which parts? In most cases, as with Tony, the entrepreneurs are people driven by above average energy and ambition and they are normally able to do everything themselves, at least for long enough to get their companies launched.

Although such versatility is a strength at the setting-up stage, it can prove a handicap when the company begins to grow. A manager like Tony Carter, who prides himself upon getting things done, has to remain willing to listen to professional advice, and follow it when it is sound. At the beginning it is better to have a man of action who doesn't mind rolling up his sleeves and getting the job done, but as the company grows it requires a more thoughtful and strategic approach from top management.

On returning to London from Florida, Tony set up office at the Institute of Directors, a stately building in Pall Mall, and hired himself a secretary, Karen Stuart. He soon found some turnkey office accommodation opposite Selfridges department store, behind Oxford street and moved in on 1 October. The only other member of the team was Mojtaba Ghassamein, a 'friend of a friend' who had been taken on to help with the selling and recruitment. The strain of doing three jobs at once meant that Tony was working twenty-four hours a day, often sleeping over in the office. He seldom got home for more than the odd weekend. His marriage finally teetered to the edge and separation proceedings soon followed.

In order to recruit people, Tony needed to be able to give them faith in the future of the company. Working from an office behind Oxford Street was not good enough, so Karen went out into the more prestigious areas, in search of some premises more suited to the image of a company which was going places. They settled on a suite in Mayfair's Albemarle Street, opposite Browns Hotel, and they moved into it a month later. The address may have been prestigious, but the premises themselves were still decidedly shabby and cramped.

Once Eric Magnuson and Ian Macdonald had left CACI it became easier for Tony to persuade other members of his old team that they should follow him. They now realized that they were under American management which believed in 'hiring and firing', and they were no longer part of a professional database consultancy because there were no figureheads left with the right image. Within three months there were ten people working there, and the main, open-plan office was overcrowded. Within ten months Ian Palmer joined the growing band of ex-CACI colleagues in Tony's new venture.

Tony had already written and printed a recruitment brochure demonstrating the seriousness of his intentions, and illustrating the differences between the new company and CACI. He had also prepared the company sales literature. He had a clear idea of where he was going, which he was able to communicate enthusiastically to potential recruits and clients. When it came down to it, however, he was selling himself as a consultant, backed up by the impressive names and facilities of DMW Inc in the States. Everybody he visited knew of Jim Martin, although many were sceptical that such a big name would be linked with such a modest 'start-up' venture.

Initially many of the sales leads came from America. When DMW and DDI in the States received requests from European companies they would send them over to Tony. He would then telephone the enquirers to find out what it was they were looking for, and prepare a brief proposal to convince them that DMW Europe could handle it.

The first sale he made was to Intel in Swindon. He was hired to consult on setting up a network throughout Europe. Tony also sold a two-week teaching contract to Fiat in Turin which he and Ian Magnuson split between them, charging £16,000. At that stage all the material was coming over from America. So Tony and Eric would be up the night before, reading the notes which they would be delivering in the classroom the following day. The results, however, pleased the clients, and their reputation started to take root.

In May, a year after the whole story had started, Tony moved out of the family home and into a flat in Earls Court, within a few yards of the tube station. Earls Court is a cosmopolitan part of West London, just a few minutes' travelling time from Mayfair. His son, Simon, who was by then at Queen Mary College at Bethnal Green, moved in with him. It was a simultaneously upsetting and exciting time for both of them.

The fourth person to join the new company was Susan, who applied to the company to be a secretary. Tony didn't give her that job but kept her details to one side. When the job of education co-ordinator came up he rang and offered it to her. After several years of working together to build the company, Susan and Tony became romantically involved. She is now the second Mrs Carter, a beautiful and charismatic woman, and the two of them were able to work side by side in the tough early years of the company's formation.

In June 1982 the first stage of start-up recruitment had been achieved and the company was up and running. There were three distinct business units within the company and there was no longer any need to be cramped into expensive West End accommodation. Although a central London address is always prestigious, the expense is impossible to justify once a company has established itself beyond a certain point, particularly in a business where the employees are nearly always visiting their clients' premises rather than the other way round. So they moved from Mayfair out to Wimbledon, a prosperous inner-London suburb, and found a home in 7,000 sq ft of office space above McDonalds and Bejam. The best part of the move was that they now had their own car park, a luxury which is virtually unheard of in the traffic-crowded city centre.

It is always hard for young companies to get started in Britain, particularly if they need to establish credit lines. Even though the offices had been empty for a long time, the landlords were still reluctant to rent them to such an unknown quantity. Because they were a young company, they were also unable to find any office-equipment supplier willing to lease them the fundamental business equipment such as office partitions, desks and chairs. So they remained open-plan and unfurnished until Arnold Edwards, the chairman of Black Arrow decided he could trust Tony and took a gamble in giving him the necessary credit, on personal guarantees from Tony and Ian Palmer.

Successful consultancy operations probably know more about the art of recruitment than almost any other type of employer. They are entirely dependent on the quality of their people for the quality of their product. If they hire mediocre people they will be a mediocre consultancy; if they don't keep those people happy they will have low morale and high staff turnovers, an expensive and destructive combination.

The JMA management has a very definite view of their company culture. They claim that whereas most companies will cite 'making money' as their core objective, they believe it should be 'having fun'. It is not as frivolous a philosophy as it sounds. The first objective of any service company must be that the people within it have professional integrity. After that come the comfort factors. If these two levels are right, then the people will start to enjoy their work. They will feel good about themselves and about their work, and that will help them to deal with any stresses which might be entailed in their jobs. If everyone within a company is enjoying themselves, and getting real job satisfaction from what they are doing, profits will automatically be generated. If the right people can be fired up with enough enthusiasm, the money will be there, provided the people and the business are well managed.

The company preaches the twin concepts of collaboration and co-operation—an open-management ideal which encourages people to talk to each other rather than sending memos, which hires people who really want to do the work, rather than those who simply have to earn a living. If people are not enjoying themselves they are probably in the wrong jobs.

Like everything else, recruiting demands careful planning. If a JMA manager can do nothing else, he has to be able to recruit well. The managers have to lean heavily on their administrative people for support, they have to know that they have the best people. The managers who are not good at selling have to recruit people who are. A manager who is good technically, billing out most of his time on a variety of projects and responsible for a business centre, has to recruit a top-notch partner to assist in marketing, selling and recruiting. That partner also has to be able to bill out some of his time as well, if the books are to balance.

Good recruiting is the first step in the growth process of a consulting company, bad recruiting is the first step in the decline of any organization.

There are three golden rules which are at the base of all recruitment decisions at JMA.

The first rule is always to hire 'partners' rather than subordinates. Most of the managers in JMA govern their own environments. They are masters of their own destinies, having the opportunities to grow business centres and to manage their own profit and loss accounts (P/L). The policy is to create semi-autonomous business enterprises, with an overall executive system for checking and auditing so that the laws of the country concerned are obeyed. They are rewarded handsomely for their success, and they are given all the guidance they want. But in the end they are allowed to do things in their own way. It would be foolish, therefore, for the directors to think in terms of managing a troop of subordinates. A sophisticated consultancy does not work like an army, and martinets will never be successful in this sort of environment. So JMA needed to recruit people who would work *with* them in growing their own worlds, not *for* them.

The second rule is to overkill *every* position; by doing this the company can be sure that it is growing from within. It is the most effective way for any organization to grow because it means that every constituent part is straining to improve, grow and fulfil its potential. The effect becomes cumulative, and the results are dramatic, if well managed.

When recruiting a data analyst, for example, the recruiter must judge whether he or she has the ability to become a project leader or a business centre manager. The process doesn't stop with managers: could a potential receptionist grow to become a secretary? The person who runs the whole wordprocessing department within the company started as a junior operator, but was recruited in the knowledge that she had the potential to do far more.

The third golden rule is never to be afraid of hiring someone better than yourself, a fear that is all too prevalent in large companies which have ceased to grow. No manager in any company should ever be afraid to recruit someone who is better than they are. Because JMA is still a relatively young organization the office politics are minimal, but in many companies it is difficult for some people to accept that others may be better than them. They feel threatened and insecure, possibly even jealous of other people's successes. Once managers have overcome this hurdle and are able to recruit above themselves, they see that their own earning potential is enhanced by their new recruit's contribution to the earnings of the group. Their status can also be raised if they gain a reputation for hiring the best people for every job.

Tony tells a story about a manager at a dinner party who passes a Russian doll to his neighbour, telling him to open it and pass on the dolls inside. Each person at the table does the same until someone ends up with the smallest doll.

'That,' says the manager, 'is what will happen to your company if you hire people smaller than yourselves.'

Tony Carter had three final questions which he asks himself when recruiting someone, and encourages everyone else to do the same:

- 'Would I buy from them?'
- 'Would I work for them?'
- 'Would I be happy to introduce them to my family and friends?'

If he has any doubts on any of these scores then he doesn't recruit.

The reasons for recruitment in a young, growing service company can be various. There may be a need for technical people to help fulfil existing contracts, project managers to oversee the delivery of contracts, managers and partners to help with growth, or administrative staff to provide the back-up needed to serve customers. No matter what the job involved, there is a basic recruitment philosophy which was formulated at the birth of the company and which still holds true, even though the company has now grown into a far more sophisticated animal. To understand the sense of the philosophies, you have to imagine them applying to a company with virtually no capital behind it, a company which existed on the quality of its people and the cash which it could generate from month to month. Obviously as it gets larger these imperatives fade somewhat, but if they are lost completely the company can all too easily lose its way and stumble.

In the first few years of the company's life a large percentage of JMA's work came from people on their 'traplines', which basically means people that the managers had met either socially or professionally, people who knew and trusted the company or an individual within a client company. The business might come direct from them, or from referrals. The same traplines worked in the recruiting process. If you have a firm of 30 people it is relatively easy to double that number in a year, since every employee is likely to know someone they would like to work with. As the company grew larger, of course, this became less practical and outside forces like recruitment agencies have to be considered if they supply a viable alternative. The basic idea of the traplines however is sound, since it requires that managers maintain contact with people who could be of value to the company in one form or another. 'People buy from people' is a truism. Traplines don't replace the need for 'cold' marketing and recruitment plans, but they provide roots from which to grow.

Recruiting the unknown, even after an extensive vetting process, is sometimes fraught with danger. During the international growth of JMA it has been necessary to recruit a number of managers in other countries. In certain cases the recruits were unknown to JMA before they were approached, and the results have not been successful. Conversely some of the big success stories have been with people who were known by the recruiter, which, in the early stages, meant Tony Carter. At this level, i.e. the top of the company, the trapline philosophy continues working for longer than it might for more easily definable job descriptions.

A recruitment trapline is simply a list of people whom the managers know and whom they believe would be interested in working with them. Maintaining the list is a continuous process, and the names on it need to be ranked in the order of the managers' requirements.

It could include known professionals in the business, either friends or people known by reputation. There are also college friends or people the managers have come across at technical meetings. Sometimes competitors can be a useful source of people, or course attendees, or former customers, or well-known industry figures.

If traplines are to be successful it is important for the managers concerned to avoid the invention of problems, and the same applies to any recruitment process. It is no good crossing someone promising off the list because 'they've only just changed jobs' or 'they won't move to London'. People and circumstances are always changing and most problems can be overcome if the potential reward is great enough. Most of the top people at JMA said 'no' to their would-be recruiter at least once and sometimes several times. In each case he persisted, planned, kept them on his trapline and overcame their objections one by one.

When high-performing professionals emerged, either at conferences, in magazine articles or through contacts, Tony got in touch with them. He sent them literature about the company and kept in contact with them, inviting them to social events at the company and keeping them informed about what was going on. He made sure that they were aware that JMA was an exciting place to work, and that they were wanted. It is very flattering for anyone to be courted so assiduously.

While the company was starting up, therefore, Tony had a tight hold on every decision, particularly in the recruitment area. As the operation grew his trapline techniques spread to other executives. The company began to recruit people who weren't automatically contacts of Tony's, nor completely in favour of his style of management.

There is always a time lapse between finding someone good and actually getting them on board. It generally takes six months for a consultancy to acquire a good person from a cold start. Most of the people worth having are happy where they are working, and have to be enticed away with a great deal of effort and planning. It is actually a good sign if someone is happy where they are, but it makes it all the harder to recruit them away.

Good managers therefore have to plan well ahead, anticipating their recruitment requirements, no matter if they arise a long time in advance. It might be a need to fulfil a new contract opportunity, to follow on an existing job or provide add-on growth to a project. It might be to fill gaps left by resignations or terminations. It is never any good waiting until the last moment and then running around trying to find someone to fill a hole. That is a sure way to hire inferior performers. In the latter two cases it is important always to think in terms of trading up, recruiting replacements who are much better than their predecessors, so that a potentially negative situation can be turned to a positive advantage.

If there is a need to recruit somebody to a well-run consultancy, that means that the money is available for their salary from the job which they are initially recruited for. It doesn't cost that much more to hire someone good rather than someone mediocre, but the potential benefits in add-on business won on the strength of the new recruit's superior performance are limitless.

One of Tony's greatest strengths was his ability to become enthusiastic about his company and products, and to infect other people with that enthusiasm. As a result he was able to attract just about everyone he wanted. At times they turned out not to be entirely happy once they were inside the company, finding the requirement to be both entrepreneurs and consultants rather too daunting, but they were nearly always keen to join because of the 'buzz' of excitement which Tony was able to generate around JMA.

As long as the managers are maintaining their traplines well then, more often than not, there are people waiting in the wings to join the company when the needs arise. In the early days there were also always several people who had signed contingency offers at any one time. As the company became richer the need for contingency offers became less apparent, since they could afford to hire good people and wait a while for the returns to come in.

Sometimes, of course, recruitment mistakes are made and in a business where the quality of your team is everything, firing becomes unavoidable. A recruiting mistake will never go away, it can only fester and while firing is probably the worst thing any manager has to do, poor performers can and must be removed. This has been particularly true at JMA with new country managers who have proved unable to bring in new contracts once the existing business in their countries has dried up. If they are kept on, the money to support them and their offices has to be found from the bottom line of other members of the group, and it generally proves to be true that if they haven't managed to win business in the first few months, the situation is unlikely to improve with time.

One of Tony's favourite quotes is: 'It is better to have a troubled ending, than to have troubles without end.' No doubt the quote was in Tony's mind during his deliberations over leaving the office of CEO to become a director.

BERMUDA – THE BIRTHPLACE OF CASE

- Every so often a new industry is born, which is destined to grow to be one of the great creators of wealth in the world.
- I-CASE is the biggest change in professional computing practice in 30 years.
- The I-CASE industry was born in Bermuda.

On Christmas Eve, 1983, Ian Palmer, his wife Glenys and their seven week-old baby were staying at Jim Martin's house in Bermuda. The house party was sitting under the twinkling lights of the Christmas tree and Glenys was laying down the law to Ian.

'Tomorrow is Christmas Day,' she was saying, 'and if you work at that computer on Christmas Day I will kill you.'

Ian replied with a dutiful 'Yes dear'.

At seven the next morning the sun rose over the Atlantic and Jim came downstairs as he always does at dawn, only to find Ian already hunched over an Apple LISA, intensely working on the methodology for performing information engineering with graphically oriented tools. Jim couldn't resist it. He had recently been divorced and his daughter was spending Christmas with her mother, the screen was a more tempting prospect than Christmas round the tree. He sat down with Ian and they both set to work as the sun grew warmer and the waves lapped on the beach below. Glenys eventually managed to drag them away for breakfast.

For some years Martin had held a growing conviction that the desktop computers with graphics could fundamentally change the way computer applications were built. Why, he kept asking, should analysts still be having to draw their diagrams with plastic templates? They should be able to draw them on a screen with the aid of a computer, collecting information, cross-checking and building a set of knowledge from which programs could be generated.

Martin had written books which had seemed startling when they first appeared, such as *Application Development without Programmers*. In them he had foreseen systems analysts working with users, with powerful computerized tools which would enable applications to be specified graphically so that code could be generated. He called this CASA/CAP (Computer-Aided Systems Analysis/Computer Aided Programming). The abbreviation was later shortened to CASE (Computer Aided Systems Engineering). What was happening in Bermuda on that Christmas Day was a first step in the birth of a new software industry.

Since 1978 Martin's friends had been coming and going from Bermuda with pieces of ideas that needed welding together into integrated software tools. A diversity of characters in the shape of software inventors had hacked away in Martin's home, arguing late into the nights about design automation.

Genius-level programmers seem to exist for much of the time in a strange world of their own, divorced from reality as most of us know it. Their heads are filled with bizarre logic and cerebral structures. Often they are avid fans of science-fiction writers, and their senses of humour seem to relate to an alien world which they inhabit.

One such friend of Martin's was John Good, an expert on palindromes. A word palindrome is a phrase or sentence in which the words are the same whether it is read forwards or backwards. He programmed his computer to scan vast amounts of text, searching for near-palindromes which could be converted into true ones. He once wrote to the Queen of England suggesting that he should be in the House of Lords because he had the world's largest collection of palindromes. When a long-suffering royal secretary wrote back asking why this was relevant, he explained that people would be able to say: 'Good Lord, here's Lord Good.'

Two of the strangest of Martin's friends were Margaret Hamilton and Zaydeen Zeldin. They were highly intellectual women who never seemed to take off their thick black stockings, no matter how fierce the Bermuda sunshine became. They would sit outside the house, lost in esoteric thought, apparently oblivious to the pink beach and lapping turquoise sea beside them. Their conversation centred on how software could be built from constructs which were mathematically provable.

Margaret Hamilton had been the executive who managed the creation of the software for the Human Landing Module of the Moon Shot project. In 1969 she watched the historic first moon landing from the NASA control room, knowing that one bug in her outrageously complex software would wreck the landing, leave the man to die on the moon, and give her an unique place in the history books. The first landing, in fact, skated very close to disaster. Margaret Hamilton and Zaydeen Zeldin, became obsessed with a technique called HOS (Higher Order Software), which was for designing software from mathematically described constructs. She and her colleagues built the technique on a DEC Vax with Martin's encouragement and money. A code generator was built to create error-free code. It was one of the first examples of computers programming computers.

The HOS corporation produced the world's first example of an integrated CASE tool, with which specifications could be expressed, converted into software design, built from provable correct constructs, and then converted automatically into executable code. The code it generated was bug-free. The corporation had a high-powered board, with representatives of two of America's most prestigious venture capital corporations, Venrock in New York and Frontenac in Chicago. The two women, however, refused to follow the advice of their board regarding the importance of marketing and of adapting the product to customer needs, and as they determinedly retained 51 per cent of the shares, they could not be budged. To Hamilton and Zeldin the mathematics and code were all-important. They believed that HOS would be a billion-dollar corporation one day, and the board meetings became stormy, with one Venrock executive literally banging his head on the boardroom table in frustration.

Ross Perot's powerful company, EDS, offered $36 million in cash to buy HOS. To the horror of the board Hamilton and Zeldin refused. Two years later HOS was bankrupt. Tony Carter chided Jim for investing in good ideas instead of investing in good people. Jim remained certain that it was possible to achieve software automation. HOS had shown that it could be done, no matter how roughly. The next attempt would benefit from the lessons learnt from HOS's mistakes.

Al Hershey from KnowledgeWare epitomized the new breed of inventor—the software inventor. Al was tall, articulate and witty. He seemed to live in a slightly foreign world, like some English-speaking planet from *Star Trek* where events all had an amusing logic of their own.

Al would settle down with the computer late at night, wearing stereo headphones, and when Martin awoke at dawn the next day, he would still be there, bleary eyed, the ashtray full of dozens of cigarette ends. He would then have to be shepherded to bed in mid-morning, after enthusiastically discussing his night's problems and accomplishments.

Like many other such geniuses, Al did not think of himself as a 'hacker', but more as an artist, inventing new forms of elegance in the computer.

Al built a product called Action Diagrammer during many such nights of one-cigarette-per-line-of-code. Action Diagrammer facilitated the visual representation and creation of code, which later evolved into one of the cog-wheels of integrated-CASE (I-CASE) tools, becoming linked to many graphical design tools with windows on the screen.

In 1982 it suddenly became much easier to create the types of diagrams that Martin wanted on the screen of a CASE tool. The Apple Corporation announced their LISA computer with LISA-Draw software. Martin spent the winter of 1982 experimenting with what he thought should be the human interfaces to future CASE tools. In more smoke-filled nights and mornings on the beach, Al Hershey started to program the new ideas, creating what would evolve into the KnowledgeWare IEW toolset.

The premier of Bermuda, John Swan, took an interest in what was happening. He had discussions with Jim about how Bermuda could stimulate clean, high-technology operations which might generate tax revenue for Bermuda like its off-shore re-insurance industry. Swan appointed a succession of ministers of technology to pursue the idea. The first of these was a top-class ocean racer with a boat of his own. The man was as tough as nails, coming from a family which dated back to the days when Bermuda was the home of pirates. The second minister was a surgeon who amputated limbs for a living and had the improbable name of Dr Stubbs. They brought Bermudans to Jim's ocean front house, to stare at computer screens. None of them realized that they were witnessing the birth of a major new industry.

In November 1983 Jim was giving a seminar on Artificial Intelligence in Washington. In the audience of 300 people was an executive from Texas Instruments, Phil Passmore. Phil was concerned about Jim's frequent references to the Japanese 'Fifth Generation' and the absence of references to what TI was starting to do with artificial intelligence. By chance Jim and Phil left Washington on the same flight. Phil was several seats behind Jim who was bent over his work as usual. Phil decided to pass a note forward to Jim on airline paper.

In the note he introduced himself and asked why TI and Jim couldn't work together to create a prototype of what he had heard Jim talking about at the conference. Jim passed a note back saying that he would be very interested in any such project.

The plane then passed through some heavy turbulence which made both men call for stiff drinks, and the note passing continued. By the end of the flight Phil had promised Jim that he would arrange for him to have the most powerful computer he needed in Bermuda, paid for by TI, and Jim would be free to do anything he wanted with it. Jim was delighted by the idea, and Phil was to prove as good as his word. He became Jim's champion within TI.

Phil was a colourful manager. Having been brought up on a ranch in Texas he now expended a great deal of energy on adopting a style as far from that of a cowboy as possible. He wore city suits and city manners. He would not be seen dead in decorated Texan boots, but still had all the Texan charm.

His father had been a southern 'preacher man', and after converting to atheism Phil was spectacularly successful at selling bibles. Now he did the selling needed to make the alien culture of CASE take hold within TI.

He became famous for his scientific approach to finding a third wife. He set himself a quota of three girlfriends a week and rated them on a Macintosh computer as one would when selecting software. The procedure caused some emotional upsets when the girls found out, but the end result was a happy and successful marriage to a warm, charming and beautiful artist.

Phil was willing to spend money on Jim's ideas. He was also a big spender in his personal life, with a taste for expensive and fast boats and a lifestyle like something straight out of *Dallas*, the soap opera. He moved quickly on his deal with Jim, bypassing the normal TI procedures. After a five-minute discussion to gain approval from two vice-presidents, John White and Roger Bate, he diverted a top-of-the-line LMI LISP computer, that was about to be shipped to TI, to Bermuda.

The day after Christmas Phil was sitting in the Mid-Ocean Club restaurant in Bermuda with two LISP machine technicians waiting for the machine's arrival, but it did not make the daily plane from Boston. For each of the next four days this scene was repeated: despite the best efforts of the freight expeditors the shipment was held up by paperwork.

After the shipment's belated arrival, Phil learned about the conflicting policies of Bermuda. In spite of the premier's efforts to encourage the increase of technology-oriented businesses, the customs officials still wanted to protect the island with a large deposit. They refused to accept either a TI cheque or Phil's credit card, so Martin wrote a cheque for

$55,000 and submitted a large expense account to TI. After a few more such problems TI refused to allow any more computers in Bermuda.

After the Bermuda government, the next obstacle was Martin's goldfish pond. The entrance to the house is via a picturesque wooden bridge over a goldfish pond. The bridge gave way under the weight of the LMI computer, depositing part of it among the startled Golden Carp.

A special electrical conduit and air-conditioning system were established in a back room of the house, which became the computer room.

Phil selected a LISP programmer, Dan Stenger, for this project. Dan had a background in developing graphics systems to support electrical engineering. He and his wife rented a home and matching pink mopeds in Bermuda. He was able to take concepts from Martin's writing and from prototypes on the LISA computer in the living room, and add computerized clockwork to them. Impressive prototypes soon became available on the large, million-pixel screen of the LISP machine.

Working in a tropical paradise does have its problems. Their progress was impeded when a giant column of ants sought refuge from a storm outside. Hundreds of thousands of them marched along the new electrical conduit and settled amidst the warm circuitry of the machine. Dan was terrified. Fortunately the local exterminator was able to attract them out without damaging the circuitry, giving a new meaning to the term 'de-bugging'.

Jim and Dan created a family of tools which were to become the basis of JMA's later relationship with Texas Instruments. The prototypes grew into TI's IEF (Information Engineering Facility), while those built in the same house with Al Hershey grew into KnowledgeWare's IEW (Information Engineering Workbench). Martin demonstrated the prototypes to the chairman and president of TI in Dallas and this stimulated a development programme on which TI eventually spent over $100 million.

At the same time the KnowledgeWare version of the prototype caused Arthur Young (the big-eight accounting firm) to agree to invest in their development. No venture capital firms were involved in these start-up operations which were destined to grow into a major segment of the software marketplace.

Around this time a close friend of Jim's, Richard Carpenter, also started a CASE company, InTech. Martin and Carpenter attempted to merge KnowledgeWare and InTech on a 50–50 basis. The obstacle was Don Brown, the president of KnowledgeWare. Carpenter and Brown could not imagine working with one another, so eventually InTech went its own way, with Martin owning a major chunk of the company.

Five years later InTech's Excelerator, KnowledgeWare's IEW and TI's IEF were clearly the three leaders in sales in the world of CASE software.

The world spends about $180 billion per year on systems analysts, programmers and their managers. The I-CASE revolution has demonstrated, so far in isolated situations, that it is possible to increase the productivity of these professionals by an order of magnitude.

Eventually, when this new technology is mature, hand-coding and debugging in languages like COBOL will be part of the quaint past, like hand-weaving of textiles in the dark mills of the Industrial Revolution. Computer professionals everywhere will plan and design their systems at a colour graphics screen with diagrams like those which emerged in the house in Bermuda.

Ever since he had joined IBM in the 1960s, Jim had been fascinated by the problems of software complexity, and he had been working to find ways of solving them.

Now that information engineering was becoming a reality, he needed to find ways of creating standards for it. Even though there would be competitive products from JMA and KnowledgeWare, and whoever else chose to enter the market, he felt they should all be working to common standards.

Jim found himself split between the two companies he had founded— KnowledgeWare and JMA. Both were setting out to produce the toolset he now knew was possible. Jim's name was attached to JMA, but KnowledgeWare might build the tools first because of Tony Carter's reluctance to invest in products. Jim backed both horses. To make sure they could work together he set out to establish common standards and for this purpose he formed a 'Politbureau' which consisted of Jim, along with the best technical people from each company—Ian Palmer and Al Hershey.

In meetings and work sessions in Bermuda the three of them did a lot of rethinking and building of prototypes. Often Jim would come up with ideas and the other two would have to force him back down because of practicalities. It was a relationship based on give and take, and mutual respect. Jim was at the time producing a book called *Recommended Diagramming Standards for Analysts and Programmers*.

The three personalities all meshed because they were all driven by the same demon, the wish to automate software development and information engineering across an enterprise. Tony Carter didn't understand a word of what they were talking about, but he liked the idea of these three tame geniuses coming together to create products which he would be able to go out and sell.

Various developers and methodologists in JMA and KnowledgeWare had to have their arms twisted to conform to the standards that were evolving in Bermuda. Steadily the CASE tools improved and became practical.

The heart of CASE tools is a repository. This is a database in which all the details are stored of the planning information, analysis models, design and coding. The repository needs to be linked to an 'intelligent' facility for checking that the information in it is completely consistent and obeys an intricate set of rules which ensure integrity. Jim and the Politbureau decided to call this intelligent repository the 'Encyclopedia'. It was essential that there should be agreement about what objects were stored in the encyclopedia, what details about them were stored, and what rules governed them. Much of the work of the Politbureau was to establish and standardize the contents of this intelligent repository.

A less Kremlin-like Politbureau one could not have imagined: Martin, the 6ft 5in futurist; Palmer, the Woody Allen-like professor; and Hershey, the witty fugitive from *Star Trek* who smoked and coded all night. Nevertheless their ideas crystallized and were obeyed in JMA, KnowledgeWare and TI. Many other CASE companies followed their standards as written up in Martin's *Recommended Diagramming Standards for Analysts and Programmers*.

In 1989 IBM endorsed the techniques of information engineering, stating that such methods are necessary to build the enterprise of the future with its many interconnected computers. IBM announced its own Repository for CASE development. This repository is essentially the KnowledgeWare one, and earns the company royalties. TI and JMA announced that they would be 'backwards compatible' with the IBM Repository. The objects in this *de facto* standard repository, and the details stored about them, are the ones that were defined by the Politbureau in Bermuda.

THE CONSULTANCY GROWS

PICKING TARGET MARKETS AND MANAGING PROJECTS

- Defining markets, identifying their needs and creating solutions to their problems.

- The creation of information engineering and winning the first big-time client.

- It is as hard to sell a project at £5,000 as at £100,000.

- If companies don't have the best decision-making tools, they will not make the best decisions.

- Use of information technology will separate the winning companies from the losing ones.

- Any service company needs an *inside salesperson* within the client organization if a sale is to be made.

JMA gradually swelled its numbers. Tony and his colleagues built up a team of people upon whom they were sure they could rely to supply the right standards of innovation and service to their clients. At the same time as undertaking their recruitment drive, however, they had to ensure that they were winning the clients who would supply the right standards of work to attract the best people. They had to decide where they were most likely to get business from, and how to make corporations want to use them.

When you first set up a company, the whole world can look like a potential client. Such a wide scope may look like a gift to the eager young entrepreneur, but in fact it can be a curse. For a new company to succeed it needs a precise target market upon which it can focus, and upon which it can concentrate all its energies. JMA's market niche consists of large multinational companies. They are the ones who most need JMA's expertise, since they are the ones with the most complicated computer systems. They are also the ones most likely to have the budgets to pay for major consultancy services, and they are the ones who can be relied on to pay their bills at the end of the day. From the consultancy salesperson's point of view they are a much more lucrative source of income since they have the money for large-scale projects.

All the same steps are needed when selling to a large company, whether it is a £5,000 or a £1 million project. It is also harder to sell small companies the idea that they need help with their technology, when they expect they should be getting that help from the suppliers, for nothing. It therefore makes sense to concentrate on people who have the money to spend. This, however, is merely an extra advantage; the reason JMA are in this market niche is because it is the world of the large mainframes, and that is where their methodologies are concentrated. Anyone with a large installation, whether it is from IBM, DEC, Honeywell or ICL, needs help with formulating their strategies.

Most of them are in the Fortune Top 500; all of them are noted for their avowed intentions to stay at the forefront of their particular industry. It is relatively easy to draw up a 'hit list' of potential customers in the right league.

The companies which have succeeded most spectacularly in the 1980s are those which dared to invest in innovation and technology. They are the ones which managed to maintain and hone their competitive edges, and they are the ones most likely to be receptive to the messages being preached by companies like JMA.

Ever since the Oil Crisis in 1974, every industry in every country has had to look at every possible way of managing its capital resources more effectively in order to extract the maximum return on investment. It has gradually become obvious to the various managements that the only way to do this is by controlling the flow of information within their companies as tightly as possible. That way they cut out wastage and maximize on every opportunity for increasing the bottom line.

The initial headlong gallop into the purchase of different computer hardware and software systems has left many senior managers gasping for breath. They have invested millions, in some cases hundreds of millions, but they still aren't getting the results they need. They are looking for people who understand what is going on, who can take a broad overview of their business problems and needs, and can show them how to achieve their goals.

There are any number of consultancies in the marketplace who are offering services of this sort, and who will take on any work which they are offered. But how can potential clients know if the consultants are going to provide what they promise? How do they know if they are as good as they say they are, or if they are trustworthy? If the clients make a mistake and hire the wrong people it could cost them a lot of money, it could also lose them enough time to fall behind the competition in some vital aspect of their business.

On the reverse side of the coin, how does a consultancy make itself known to clients? How does it reassure them that it is going to be around for long enough to take on major projects, that its people are the best, that they are trustworthy?

The answer is that a consultancy needs to have a good reputation. But how do you get the first jobs upon which to build a reputation? In order to convince people that they should take you on before you have a reputation, you need to be able to convince them that you, and only you, can answer their most pressing problems, which means that first you must identify what they are.

Most senior managers in any client company are looking for the answers to a number of similar crucial questions. Is their IT investment being made in the right application areas? Can IT improve their ability to compete, and is it doing so? Does their current computing and communications resource provide a sound platform for future business expansion? Can the information management organization adapt to new technologies? Is the core business application adequately managed, and is it accessible to those who must use it? How can they maximize the return on the total IT investment?

They are looking for help from people who understand what all these questions mean. They want people who have a broad experience of other companies and their problems, who can bring new perspectives to old problems. Although JMA was new and inexperienced, the people it was employing were all widely experienced in answering the right sorts of questions for clients.

In essence, two key issues have to be resolved in most large organizations. The investment in IT must complement the company's business strategy, and the IT infrastructure must be closely integrated, yet flexible. It must be characterized by readily accessible working data, efficient communications, sufficient computing resources and a rational organizational structure.

These were exactly the sorts of questions which JMA was setting out to answer for clients. The team was increasingly confident that it could do it — it just had to convince the clients of the fact.

The JMA team were offering consultancy and training services for information policy and strategy, information engineering and tele-communications and IT infrastructure.

The consultants, for instance, could define a client's IT policy, through detailed analysis of their information needs and the ways in which that information flows within the organization. They could then make practical recommendations on the computing, software and communications resources requirements. In many cases the senior management within the client company is insufficiently involved in the information management process. As a result data processing, communications, factory automation and office automation have been developed separately and the issue of whether to centralize or decentralize has distracted management from taking the vital decisions. This leads to crucial applications being neglected.

The consultants can then interpret the client's business objectives into a matching information and communications strategy, and make clear definitions between what are data and what are business processes. They can define a workable IT infrastructure for the company (computers, workstations and communications networks), and define the information and communications strategy in relation to the enterprise's external environment (markets, sub-contractors etc). They can improve the relationship between the IT organization and the system user, and enhance the latter's role in the system development life-cycle. They can automate the automation process and apply a complete method as the foundation for this process.

Because of their experience and technical backgrounds the consultants are able to evaluate the potential for IT within the framework of the client's corporate strategy. Or they can formulate a strategy and detailed plan which would include technical features, for the implementation of information and communications systems. They can organize and manage the information flow, including the communications infrastructure and the services it provides. They can design computer-based information systems, evaluate and select third-party products and services and implement automated systems development facilities.

Although virtually every organization of any size needs to address exactly these problems if it is to survive in the coming years, there are only a limited number of companies in the world who will:

1. understand the value of such a service;

2. have the political will to employ it; and

3. have the resources to pay for it.

A survey in the mid-1980s tried to differentiate between the leading and lagging companies in the world, demonstrating how the leading companies employed information technology and the laggers didn't. In many cases it was possible to tell the difference between the two groups simply in the titles which they gave to the managers and departments concerned. Those that were talking about 'information processing' were likely to be winners, whereas those who were still talking about 'data processing' were likely to still be thinking of computers as a way of monitoring things that were past, rather than using information to see where to go in the future.

Those who had data processing managers reporting to financial directors were among the laggers, whereas those who had chief inform-ation officers who were on the board, understood that information systems should be a profit centre to be built upon, not a cost centre to be controlled. The difference is typified by American Airlines, where the chief information officer is on the board, and whose information processing department contributes more to the bottom line than any other part of the operation. In the banking and financial services sector the same is true. The new products which are springing up are in the service areas, and they are based on the use of information and technology to sell to the outside world.

All the most successful big companies now understand the value of information systems. It is a multi-billion pound industry, watered by multinational organizations who have a continuous need for consultancy services. Most of them have the political will to use consultancies like JMA, although not all of them have the organizational abilities to do so.

By January 1982 the work was beginning to flow in for Tony and his team. The jobs at Intel and Fiat were followed by a long-running contract with Chevron and then a prestigious job with BP at Britannic House in London's Moorgate.

With the company up and running, Tony and his new recruits were selling as hard as they could. They were working their traplines for all they were worth, following up all the people they knew from their past dealings, and who they believed would trust them with new contracts if they knew they were in the market. Tony himself had several contacts at BP from his past and he courted them assiduously.

BP had its own software house, Scicon, which worked on their database strategy. Tony and his team were asked to come in and critique the strategy. Tony had won the account against competitive bids, by promising to provide John Bennet, a well-known database man at IBM, and John King, an articulate, walking encyclopedia from California, who flies his own plane and absorbs computer knowledge like a vacuum cleaner.

As usual Tony had to promise the people before he had them on board, and ensure that they were available to him the moment the project was due to commence. John Bennet came on board on a Monday morning and by nine o'clock was in BP's offices. John King was flown in from San Francisco and only given enough time to change his clothes in Tony's office, before being sent down to Moorgate. Together with Tony himself, this was the complete team.

At that stage Tony was buying John King's time from Dixon Doll, just like any other customer, a situation which was to become a huge bone of contention later in the relationship. DMW charged their people out to Tony at their normal rates, but Tony was able to get more for them, with hard selling. Even at that stage he was getting up to £1,000 a day for the top consultants, which was just below the top rates being charged by some of the competitors. Although good clients will never complain about paying if they think they are getting value for money, getting the mark-ups high enough to make it worth bringing people over from the States was hard work.

The entry into BP was the first serious, strategic job for the young consultancy, a very different prospect from the teaching work they had been doing up until then. When you are teaching you simply arrive on the allotted day and put in the agreed amount of time. With strategic consulting you have to have the confidence to put your hand on your heart and say 'this is what we believe', even if your beliefs upset the client. If you are simply telling them what they want to hear you are no use to them. Nor was it enough to tell them that their database strategy was no good; the consultants also had to be able to recommend a course of action.

At that stage the company still did not have the ability to produce the long, smooth, prestigious in-house reports which many bigger consultancies were creating. Instead, they concentrated on writing the best reports available in the marketplace, and had them produced out-of-house. When it came to the final presentation to the senior management at BP, Tony arrived with all their beautifully presented work parcelled up in a pair of carrier bags from Boots the Chemist, BP accepted the recommendations, and signed a long-term contract. They employed John Bennet for a year, which meant that the consultancy was inside their first major customer, and was able to start building it into a major account.

Once consultants are working within a major client company, the next thing which they have to be taught to do is recognize other business opportunities within the organization. By the time they are working inside a client they have established a reputation, if only a very localized one, and they have to capitalize on it in every way they can. It is also impractical to expect a consultant who is working on a major project to have any time for marketing and selling the consultancy's services to other companies. If business is to grow from that consultant it has to be grown from the existing client.

There is a temptation for consultants to hide themselves away from the client and get on with the job. If new business is to develop from existing projects, however, clients have to be cultivated. Tony trained his team to spend time with the clients and get to know their worlds, their problems and their needs. He would encourage them to do the clients' staff work for them, to win their confidence and make them reliant on the consultancy. If, for instance, a consultant has helped a client to prepare a few graphs for his or her budgeting project, the consultant would then have a fairly good idea of what the money was going to be spent on the following year.

Inside every client organization is an inside salesperson. These are the people who need to employ the consultant in order to achieve their own goals, whatever they might be. They are therefore the consultants' champions. They battle with the corporate bureacracy which is unfamiliar territory for the consultants, and convince sceptical boards of directors that it will be money well spent. The consultants have to look after their inside salespeople in every way they can. The more successful the inside salespeople become the more they will rely on the back-up which they have received, and the more ready their superiors will be to accept their recommendations for future contracts with the consultancy.

Consultants must give their clients the means to be successful, and visibly so. They need outstanding executive summaries which explain how the project can be successful, which they can show to their bosses. They need evidence to prove to everyone else that they have made a good decision in hiring the consultancy, and that the job is being done effectively.

Once inside a large organization, consultants also need to generate referrals. The more people they meet within the organization the better idea they will get of their needs, and the more opportunities they will unearth for the consultancy. This is another form of 'trapline', a term which works equally well as both a recruitment and selling technique. It basically means using contacts to lead to more contacts. Within a large client organization it can work particularly well, since new contacts feel comfortable with a company which already understands its own corporate philosophy and culture, and which has already proved itself in the field. Such a company is not taking a jump into the dark and hiring an unknown quantity. An internal referral leapfrogs many of the barriers to purchase which face a consultant selling into a company for the first time.

At planning sessions the consultants can ask for as many names as possible of people to whom they should talk in order to understand the business. There are also budget cycles which can be exploited. In many companies, executives who do not spend their budgets one year will have them cut the following year. So when consultants know that a fiscal year is drawing to a close they can find out who has money which has not yet been spent.

From February 1982 to March 1983, Tony had a dozen people working on the BP account, and six years later JMA was still helping BP.

Once a client has been won, the majority of a consultant's time is taken up with project management. Assuming that the recruitment and sales sides of the business are going well, the next ingredient of success is bringing the project to fruition, and making it lead to new business. That requires the application of some sound management principles.

Whether they are selling education courses, products or consultancy time, project management is JMA's bread and butter. It provides the bulk of their revenue and profit. If projects were to go wrong, and clients refused to pay, it would wipe out the company's bottom line. Sound management is their business.

Any consultants who think that they don't have to worry about delivering a project until the last day are likely to run into trouble along the way. Consultancy is a service industry and, as such, must provide a continuous service to customers, something that can be seen and judged at every stage.

When customers first visit an expensive restaurant the management do not wait until the end of the meal, when the diners are sitting with heavy stomachs and light heads, before delivering the service. If the meal is to be a success it must consist of a whole series of satisfactions. The first will be the impression which the room makes on the customers as they walk in. If it makes the customers feel good they will sit down in a confident mood. It continues with the design and layout of the menu and the way in which the waiters treat the customers. Each course is then judged on its own merits. Does it look good? Do the customers look forward to the taste? Does it taste as good as it looks? Do they feel ready for the next course afterwards? Do they feel the wines they are drinking with each course are right? Do they feel confident that the waiters are advising them on the best wines, not just the most expensive?

In just the same way the delivery of a consultancy project starts with the proposal, or menu. A good proposal will help to prepare both the consultancy team and the client for what lies ahead. It sets the standards and makes the promises. A bad one will promise too much, like a menu which is written too pretentiously for the food which is going to be served up, making it impossible for the supplier to deliver successfully. If the wrong promises are made they will end up costing money, destroying reputations and damaging prospects for add-on business. If the diners leaving the restaurant feel that they did not receive the meal which they were led to believe they would enjoy, they will probably haggle over the bill, and they certainly won't return or recommend any of their friends to go there.

A good proposal, therefore, must contain the right 'background', just as a good menu must be written by a chef who knows about the food he or she is creating. This is where the consultants show that they know the clients, their business and their problems. It is like a doctor and patient relationship. If the patient doesn't believe that the doctor understands the illness which has brought them together, hasn't listened to the symptoms and hasn't put them into the context of other ailments, then the chances are that the patient will have no faith in any remedy which the doctor might prescribe. The background quoted in the proposal may simply be the result of one conversation with the potential client, but it will include a statement of what is being done, what the problem is that needs to be solved, and what the requirements are. It talks also about how the client is responsible for the requirement which has given the consultant the opportunity to work within that organization. The client's mind has therefore been put at rest regarding the consultant's understanding of the problem; they can both now concentrate on the solutions to be found.

A consultancy always needs to look for ways to encourage a client to go for an early start, while the problems are still fresh in everyone's mind, and while the enthusiasm for the project is still running high. If people are allowed to procrastinate about starting up a project, other more pressing, short-term problems may arise and distract attention from the long-term needs. By building in a sense of urgency to the proposal, the consultancy can help to provide some momentum to the project. They also need to begin to build a case which explains why that particular consultancy is the only one which is equipped to handle the project. Obviously the clients are going to expect every consultancy to say that, but if the arguments are sound they can still be convinced. To do that the proposal will discuss relevant previous work which helps to establish the company's unique capability to handle the project. It is vital that the background is clear in both the consultant's and the client's minds if the job is to be successful and if all misunderstandings that might arise later are to be avoided.

The proposals provide the inside salespeople with the ammunition they need to convince their organizations that they should hire JMA. Inside salespeople are nearly always in a position of having to justify their budgets to someone, and have to demonstrate that their project is the one which would be the most useful allocation of funds. The proposals therefore need to contain something about JMA's capabilities, since they are being read by people who may know nothing about the company, but they have to be short enough to be readable. They have to explain why they will need certain areas of expertise to achieve the desired results, and will then go on to convince them that all those levels of expertise exist within JMA. The proposals are full of statements starting off with 'JMA is uniquely qualified to...'.

During a project there a number of what the JMA managers call *deliverables*. Like the meal in the restaurant, the deliverables are extremely important to the clients, as they tell them what they will be getting for their money. Normally when someone goes shopping they know exactly what they are going to be buying. With consultancy work this is not always the case.

Returning to the restaurant analogy, the customers who walk into a restaurant for the first time do not know what sort of meal they are going to get. The name and style of the restaurant will give them some clues and will tempt them in initially. The menu will then give them another clue, and if properly presented will make them feel confident to continue. They will then, however, judge each course and each drink as it comes. At the end of the meal they might make a sweeping overall judgement as to whether or not the restaurant lived up to its promise, but at each stage of the meal they will be making interim judgements on what has been put in front of them.

If clients are spending £100,000 on consultancy services they are going to need constant reassurances that they are getting what they are paying for. They are not going to want to wait until the end to make a judgement on whether or not it was the right solution for their problems. They therefore need to start with a list of the things they are going to get for their money. Before promising a deliverable, however, the consultants must be sure that it is within their power to produce the goods. It is no good promising *nouvelle cuisine* and then serving fish and chips. There is a temptation in any consultancy business for a bad consultant to promise the clients whatever it is that they want to hear, regardless of whether it is actually the best course for them to follow. Once they have won the contract with a set of fine proposals which make the client glow with anticipation, the consultants then look for ways in which to make good their promises, and usually end up having to find excuses for why they are failing instead. It is not long before such consultancies gain bad reputations.

The JMA consultants plan to make all the progress briefings which they hold with the clients into specific deliverable items. Meetings of any sort help to keep the clients involved and give the consultants the opportunity to discuss the projects with them in depth. Face-to-face discussions take out the need for cumbersome reports and give the clients a high level of satisfaction. It is always better to make personal contact with someone than give them a report which they can't question, and which can only be expanded upon with a great deal of extra work and time. When writing reports for clients there is always a temptation for a bad consultant to make them longer and more complicated than they need to be, simply to reassure the clients that a lot of work is under way. The result may be that the client will either not bother to read it at all, in which case it is a waste of time, or will become baffled and irritated by the complexity of it, and will demand a meeting to clarify what it all means anyway.

If clients are able to ask direct questions they will feel much more confident that they are getting the answers they need, and the consultants will be able to get a direct feedback on their ideas, which will help to keep them on track and avoid going off at tangents which seem relevant at the time but which are not part of the overall direction which the client needs.

Having put together the list of deliverables, the consultants sit down and go over them with the clients, making sure that the list contains the things they need, and that everyone's expectations are the same. If there are any misunderstandings they are cleared up at this stage, since they can only lead to wasted time and effort if allowed to continue.

In planning the deliverables the consultants also plan for new business growth, and look for ways in which they can give the clients a satisfaction very early in the project.

Planning for growth means planning to put extra people on the project and to build in add-on business by clearly demonstrating the worth of the project to the client early on. If inside salespeople can be shown that they have made a right decision in hiring the consultancy, and that the results are going to be as good, or even better, than expected, then they are going to want to find other ways of achieving good results. Giving the inside salespeople early satisfaction also means giving them something tangible to show to their bosses. It might be a briefing demonstrating what they are trying to achieve. It might be an executive summary of what has been accomplished. It might be a report on the successful design phase. Whatever it is it must demonstrate that the consultancy is as good as its word, and is providing the client with something which will produce very tangible benefits.

During the first few months of a long project the consultants need to convince the inside salespeople that it is, and will continue to be, a success. The inside salespeople need to be armed with a constant supply of ammunition to give their bosses; it can't be allowed to dry up after the first 'satisfaction'. It is their kudos which is at stake, not the consultants', when they go to their bosses and say 'Look how much we have done.' If this can be achieved they will be more willing to talk about add-on business at an early stage. If the inside salesperson's boss catches him or her unawares by asking what it is these consultants are doing for their money, and it takes a week to come up with some evidence of activity, there will be a serious dent left in the consultancy's credibility and the inside salesperson will have a harder time convincing anyone that the consultants should be hired for more work later on.

Once the consultants and clients both know what they have got to accomplish, they get together to decide on their work statement and technical approach. This is simply a matter of gaining a clear idea of what is to be done and how it will be achieved. This is written as a goal- and process-orientated statement, e.g. 'In the first three months we shall design. In the second three months we shall build prototypes. In the third three months we shall review.'

No unnecessary details are given at this date, but both the consultants and the clients must have the same expectations if the project is to succeed.

A minimum proposal needs to be produced, since most client companies have in-house processing departments. In addition to differentiating what they, the consultancy, will bring to the client company, they want to give them a proposal which helps them to appreciate the complexity of the problem. In other words they want to explain that 'there are nine ways of tackling this problem, but only an expert such as ourselves will know which is the right way'. The proposal doesn't tell them which is the right way, but points out how difficult some of the technical problems to be solved are.

What is needed is a good goal- and process-orientated statement with which the clients will feel comfortable. Because they have a detailed list of deliverables they know what they are going to get, which takes care of any dissatisfactions they might have about any aspects of the proposal.

Planning for growth is always vital, and the consultants will write the first task of the add-on into the statement. In this way they are helping to ensure that they will get it. Under the headings 'Recommendations for the future' the consultants are actually writing their next proposal; e.g. 'Other analyses needed are...'. By coming up with a list of recommended applications for this project in the task statement, the consultants are more likely to get the add-ons earlier, sowing the seeds in the client's mind, preparing them for the idea of even greater benefits and rewards which can be achieved in the future. Technology is a fast-developing area; there is always going to be more that any client can do to improve their use of information. The secret is to get them used to the idea of continuous updating and improvement, and not to allow them to believe that they can just 'do a project' and then sit back and do nothing further for another five years. To do that the clients have to be able to see just how much they will gain from a policy of continuous development and how much they will lose by not having one.

The consultants will always prepare a schedule at this stage. This is important since it will take into account possible hitches. There is a tendency for good consultants to say proudly 'we can get that done for you in two weeks', which allows no time for their families or themselves to fall sick, their cars to break down or for something to go wrong on another project. If they actually have to commit themselves to a schedule they are more likely to ensure that they give themselves enough spare time, and don't end up disappointing the client with a late delivery.

If a consultancy promises to deliver on Tuesday and then doesn't deliver until Friday, they are inefficient and ineffective in the eyes of the client. If they had promised Friday week and delivered it a week early, then they would be heroes.

A late delivery will embarrass the inside salespeople, who have staked their reputations on the performance of the consultancy, and if everyone starts rushing to meet a deadline the work may become slipshod. The resulting drop in morale and reputation would start a snowballing effect, with both staff and clients leaving to do business elsewhere. An early delivery leaves plenty of time for fine tuning and for marketing the add-ons.

Schedules have to be worked out in detail with the project team. Project managers need to cross-check their judgements. They are hiring top-class professionals and need to make sure they utilize them through consultation, and respect their judgements. The whole team consequently becomes committed to the schedule. If they had an in-put into agreeing it, they then have a vested interest in making sure it is adhered to. If the project manager prepares the schedule single-handed, and then just tells the team what they are going to be doing, they have instantly been turned into subordinates instead of partners, and will start to act in a very different, and less effective way.

It is always important for a consultant to allow for flexibility in a schedule. Tasks need to be overlapped so that those that go well and finish early will not leave holes in the revenue flow while you are waiting for the next stage to start.

Consultancies often have a number of projects which are beginning and ending at different times, with the consequent need to accelerate or slow down on a project. By overlapping tasks the consultants can do a better job and are able to produce much more impressive reports.

Instead of saying, 'At the end of the quarter we finished task one and began work on task two', they can write, 'During this quarter progress was made on tasks 1, 3, 7, 9 and 12.' It may have required exactly the same levels of effort, but it reassures the client that this project is being dealt with properly and thoroughly.

A JMA project team always becomes involved in the project plan. Commitment is sought from all the relevant people on the team and a chart is drawn up for internal use, demonstrating flexibility to use substitutions, to bring in new people, etc. A consultancy project is always a process of evolution, which means that the team who start to work on it may not be the right people to finish it. Other jobs may also come up during the project, on which certain members of the team would be better employed. There is no advantage to be gained from rigidly holding together the original unit of people.

Key people in the team can seldom be promised to clients for 100 per cent of the time. They are usually needed on other projects. They are high value items and have to be priced as such. If they ended up working all the time on a small project with no add-ons it would be a result of bad planning. On big contracts, of course, it is different.

The project manager needs to be identified early in the planning stage. The client wants to know who will be handling the job, as does the project team. An early decision will help to settle everyone in and will focus expectations.

The actual contract vehicle needs to be got right, particularly in the US. There are two main types of contract which JMA works with. There is the sort which allows for time and material, and another which is fixed price. Any proposal assumes some specific legal arrangement between JMA and the client organization.

the aim is to start the project with a client satisfaction, and with the clients holding realistic expectations of what they will be receiving in the way of service. By the first day of the project the project managers are already about a third of the way through their job. They have done the scheduling and staffing, and the tasking is all laid out. They have already done 10 per cent of their add-on marketing. They have created favourable client expectations, an early, visible product and Task One of their add-on.

Any consultancy which wants to build a reputation must deliver what it proposes. There is a contractual arrangement with the client, so it is no good delivering something different, but it is vital to deliver the spirit of the contract as well as the letter. Everyone on a project team has to be fully conversant with the proposal and what it promises if they are going to be sure they are working towards a common goal. It is also important to know what the contract does not cover, so that if the client says 'While you are here could you just take a look at this other problem?', everyone on the consultancy team knows whether it is included in the contract or not. If it isn't then they have to prepare another proposal to cover the new work.

A funded project is an asset to a consultancy, and the consultants have to ensure that they receive a return from their asset, in which they are investing their time. First they have to cultivate the clients, finding out about their world, their problems and their needs. It is a temptation for consultants who are not necessarily good communicators to just keep their heads down and get on with the job. This is a mistake, hiding away from the clients or working on without talking to them is counter-productive. A relationship of mutual trust and respect needs to be built, as it is important that the clients should grow to rely on the consultants in as many ways as possible.

The consultants must make the clients 'look good'—that is what they have been hired for. If the inside salesperson is seen as the instigator of a thoroughly successful project, it is more likely that the consultancy will be hired to do the same again later.

While working for one person within an organization, the consultants are also generating referrals to other people, building up their traplines. At planning sessions the consultants need to ask who else they should talk to in the company in order to understand more fully what happens, and then make sure that they do talk to those people, and acquaint them with the work which is under way. They should also be aware of the client's budget cycles, so that they can talk to them towards the end of their fiscal year about how much money is left to be spent.

During the course of a project, the JMA consultant remains constantly alert to any opportunities that may arise to develop new products or to acquire existing products from clients. It is often possible for consultants to use their client environments to locate the market for a new product which will be mutually beneficial.

Everyone who works on a consultancy project from JMA is being continuously developed both technically and from the entrepreneurial point of view. The project manager is doing add-on marketing, for instance, being the one who is interfacing with the client every day. Everyone in the team is given responsibility from an early date. They are challenged to perform and their progress is monitored.

To ensure that they are heading in exactly the right direction, a draft of the final report is prepared on the first day of the project, noting what is to be delivered on the last day. The problems which need to be solved are never again as clear as they are on the first day. All project activity can then be screened on the basis of its contribution to the final report or project deliverables. By using this management tool the consultancy avoids falling into the trap of laying beautiful preparations without ever actually getting anything done.

At this stage there is already enough material available to prepare a progress chart, task schedule, task-manning and sub-tasking milestones.

The milestones are all tangible. Rather than saying, 'Give me two weeks to think about it', consultants will say 'Give me two weeks to write an outline of that.'

The progress chart then acts as an early-warning system in case something is taking too long or costing too much. Sometimes technical problems do not get solved as quickly as expected and require extra manpower in order to stay on course. Any deviations of this sort can be spotted on a chart and rectified before they throw the whole project off schedule. The chart will also allow the consultants to be able to demonstrate to clients exactly how their money is being spent and to explain why they need to buy add-on services later.

Each week there is a project meeting to ensure that no one forgets what it is they are supposed to be doing, and loses sight of the schedule. It is easy for a consultant who is wrapped up it the day-to-day business of the client to forget that there are other people working on the same project who could help out with problems. The project leaders need to know what each person is doing in order to ensure that the team's energies are being channelled in the most useful directions. They need to be able to spot problems as they occur, which can only happen by talking to members of the team, and they need to keep everyone motivated.

The JMA managers insist that everyone involved in a particular project attends the meetings. They are held at a regular time and the manager will make anyone who fails to turn up feel extremely bad. Everyone has to speak. The technical people talk about what they have accomplished in the last week and what they intend to do in the next week. They talk about their problems and how they solved them, since their solutions might be useful to other people.

Add-on tasks are discussed, since the people working closely with the project understand the client's needs better than anyone else. They know what should be done in the future and what the client is likely to be willing to pay for. An add-on task-log is prepared while the project is under way. If people know that they are going to have to speak at the meetings, they will put more thought into what they are going to say, which means they are giving more thought to how they could help the client in the future.

By having regular meetings, the consulting team can review and criticize their own work, and solve the problems before the client even has to find out about them. To be successful a review system has to be organized to run all the time, not just when a crisis has arisen. Other experts from within the consulting company who are not actually working on the project team are called in regularly to give an outside perspective the work. The project might even be signed off by Jim Martin himself.

At the beginning of a project the team prepares a list of reasons why they will need to talk to the client during the course of the work. The client needs to know what is going on at all stages. Clients never like surprises, and good management means that none arise. They are made to feel confident that the work agreed on is going ahead. If something different is needed, then they are told about it and prepared for it.

Every meeting with the client is a marketing opportunity for the consultants. Only by talking to the clients can they find out what is happening and changing in their world, and how this is likely to affect their needs, and the way in which the consultants can help them. Clients' needs can often change radically during the course of a project. The change might be caused by a technical breakthrough, or because of the addition of further business. The consultants want to help with these changes in any way they can. They want to help the inside salespeople to do their staff work, so that when they get questions from their bosses they are able to give detailed and technically correct answers.

The golden rule of success on any project work, however, is to 'finish things'. It is all too easy for a consultancy to become involved in an endless process of 'getting ready'. Successful completion of a job usually comes down to getting things right the first time and then doing them. The saying which JMA managers like to quote is 'How come there's never time to do it right, but there's always time to do it over?'

It helps if at the beginning of the planning stage, the managers ensure that they leave themselves enough time to do a thorough job. Tight, self-imposed deadlines can lead to rushed and sloppy work as the team desperately battles with the clock. If possible they show the project findings to the clients before the final deadline and ask if they would like to see any fine-tuning before the final delivery.

By filling in the outline of the final report at every stage of the project, the team ensures that the project is constantly being marched towards its conclusion. The clients were satisfied when they bought the project, otherwise they wouldn't have signed up. They must remain confident that the consultancy is going to deliver what they promised. They are not interested in much else, expect when they are next going to be given satisfaction.

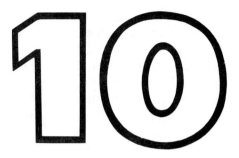

BECOMING
MULTINATIONAL

- How to pick the right international markets.

- Finding and motivating the right international entrepreneurs and managers.

- Only open an overseas office when you have the business to support it.

- Find entrepreneurs who can build companies from nothing, and motivate them to manage the companies as if they were their own.

By the end of the first year the team was beginning to grow and take on a recognizable shape. The connection with James Martin was invaluable, but the UK team were also able to compete for business on their own merits. Where Martin's reputation proved particularly valuable was in emphasizing the importance of a project to a client company's own management. When Tony won a contract for a strategic study for ICL, he was able to involve both Dixon Doll and Jim in the job. Jim flew over to Britain, acting as a catalyst to bring all the senior managers at ICL together. The fact that someone of Jim's calibre felt it worth while coming in on the project demonstrated to them that it was worth their while to take time to listen.

The team was getting into the right sorts of companies, and not only in the UK. In Holland they were working for IBM and Philips. At Philips they were advising management on the strategies they should adopt in order to succeed in America. Jim flew over for a three-day workshop with the new Philips CEO and the worldwide presidents of Philips companies. These were big-time contracts from companies who were not afraid to pay the prices which Tony was asking, so long as they achieved the results they were looking for.

The success of the company meant that Tony was recruiting new people well ahead of plan, which meant that more money was being spent than anticipated, because the growth of business to be served was also ahead of plan. The £50,000 loss which he had predicted for the first year had ended up as a £90,000 loss, although revenue was up £15,000 above the predicted £450,000.

Both Dixon and Jim were impressed by Tony's performance, and were not worried by the extra losses in the first year. They could see why they were happening, and they could see that the company was in a strong position to move forward. There was no question now that the work was there and that the people Tony was able to attract were in demand. It was really just a question of how to control the growth so that the company remained on solid ground and did not grow too far too fast.

Tony's European operation was doing incomparably better than Dixon's company in America. Tony understood the delicate balancing act of labour utilization and mark-up rates which are the downfall of so many consultancy companies. They felt they were in safe hands.

In the second year the company could comfortably have moved into profit, but Tony didn't want to stop there, having seen the potential for growth in other countries like Holland, he wanted to open up geographically, including the States. He chose to put money into setting up companies in Sweden, Italy, Holland, Ireland, France, Australia and America.

A consultancy working at these high corporate levels, preaching the creeds that they preached, had to be multinational. Going international is also exciting and keeps a consultancy up-to-date. Consultants have to be ahead of the game if they are to be worth hiring, which means they must know what is happening at the leading edge of their industry, wherever in the world that edge is. Tony never saw an alternative to opening up in other countries—there was no alternative. The only question was: which was the best way to do it? He and his managers were already working at full stretch. To start living on airplanes and battling with the recruitment/marketing cycle in other lands and other languages might well have caused the elastic to snap.

There are two ways of opening up new markets. You can either decide that you want to move into a particular country and set about finding someone in the country who can handle it (this happened in Sweden, Italy, Ireland, USA, France and Hong Kong), or else you find that you are handling a number of large projects in a particular country, which makes it relatively straightforward to open a local office and start looking for more business in the same area, taking on some local people to help handle it (as happened in Holland, Singapore and West Germany).

When an enquiry initially came in from a country where the company did not yet have a presence, Tony did not encourage consultants to immediately jump on to airplanes to go and see the enquirer. That approach can lead to a great deal of wasted time and money. The first step was to talk to them on the telephone to find out some vital facts. Are they, for instance, in a position to buy consultancy services now? Do they have the budget for that sort of activity? Do they have the authority to spend it?

The enquirer would then be encouraged to come to see JMA, since that was where all the relevant material was to hand, and once the project was definite a team of people would start visiting the site.

If a project in a new country began to build into something more solid and lasting, and there was someone in the country whom the JMA directors believed had the entrepreneurial abilities to build a company, then they would think about opening an office and going after new clients. In this way the company has spread across Europe and into the States. Some countries, however, simply do not have large enough markets to support a full-sized operation and any accounts won within those countries will be handled from an existing office. Some markets, such as Singapore, appear to have the potential for an office, but when explored prove hard to grow. The opportunistic approach which the group took at the beginning is now being tempered with hard-earned experience.

Tony then took a very definite viewpoint on how to conduct the overseas offices which sprang up as a result of his policies, and it was encapsulated in one phrase—'*The Country Manager is King*'.

To begin with this was as simple as it sounded. Once he had found somebody who he thought was good enough to open up a branch of JMA in a new country, he gave them a small bit of capital (say around £10,000), some shares in the company and, if they were lucky, the income from whatever business was already up and running in that country. From then on they were independent in their decisions and the paths they followed as long as they embraced the mission of selling information engineering. That philosophy continued for as long as Tony was in the driving seat, although it gradually had to be set against the growing need for each country to conform to the group's overall positioning statements, missions and goals. There soon had to be a policy manual, by which they all had to live.

The important part of the start-up equation is the business which already exists, since that will be paying the salaries of the country manager and whatever team is in place from the start. It was bound to take time to build up a new client base, as it had done in Britain, and during that time a company does not want to be haemorrhaging money. If there is some existing business, it also means that by the time that initial contract is finished it will be obvious whether the new country manager is capable of winning more, either with new clients or add-on business, or whether the appointment has been a mistake and needs to be terminated before it starts to cost the group serious amounts of money.

As a general rule Tony believed in giving each of the new start-up entrepreneurs a year to prove that their business plans were going to work. The idea of the start-up money was simply to give them something in the bank to begin with. For the first three months they were left to find their own feet, with little more than a friendly weekly telephone call enquiring how things were going and whether there was anything which they needed help with. If a major decision like the renting of an office was involved then Tony might visit them to look it over.

In the second three months the new entrepreneur would probably be invited to come over to London for a day, to help them see what was going on and to get a feel for the group which they were becoming part of. While the first three months involved the setting of general directions, they could now talk about more specific objectives like where the orders were going to be coming from, and which people looked as if they would be coming onboard. In some cases there might be some extra help offered in the way of translating brochures or providing back-up staff.

In the third three months the holding company managers started trying to understand whether or not the new venture was going to work, so that they could lay plans for the following year. At this stage they would be able to talk positively about the things that they would be able to do. By the fourth quarter of the first year they would know if the venture was not going to work, and they could be looking at ways of separating with the minimum of pain on all sides. When an operation doesn't work out it is generally no one's fault, it simply means that the wrong people had a go.

A man called Jean-Marc Baugier tried to open France in exactly this way. He had come from IBM and Tony felt that he was worth trying. The business just didn't develop and Jean-Marc decided that he would be better suited to working simply as a freelance consultant.

In Italy Tony went into business with Lorenzo Bozio, a very competent manager and salesman with whom he and Ian Palmer had worked at CACI when he was general manager for Sperry. Tony had met Lorenzo on the rugby field, when Lorenzo was playing for Italy and Tony for the Public School Wanderers. This was a 50–50 deal. Lorenzo, however, later decided that he wanted to continue marketing products which the rest of the group was not going to be able to handle due to clashes of interest. He bought out Tony's 50 per cent and went on by himself.

In Australia they set up an operation with three consultants who recruited themselves a boss called Les Adams. Les and Tony did not get on from the start. Tony felt so strongly about the man that he cut all ties with the Australian operation. Although Tony supported Ian Palmer's plans in trying to get new operations going in Australia, Singapore and Hong Kong in the following years, it wasn't until after Tony left the company that Jim found another contact to take JMA into the potentially lucrative Australian market.

As the company grew the Country Manager is King philosophy had to be tailored only slightly. There soon had to be some central controls over things like pricing and marketing, otherwise you could have the ridiculous situation of clients in one country being able to buy JMA services more cheaply in another country, even though the consultancy is up and running in their own home town. But given those few perameters, the philosophy continued to hold true until Tony's demise in 1989. If entrepreneurs could convince the holding company that they could set up new national branches of JMA, they were left to do it in their own way, even if that way wasn't exactly the way Tony would do it himself. If they succeeded, then they knew that they had done it all alone. If they failed they had no one to blame but themselves.

The first spectacular success was in the Netherlands. Tony had always had a strong base in Holland, right from his days at CACI when he had had a seventy-person operation in Amsterdam. JMA had found an equal degree of success there although they initially handled the business from the UK. With the contracts at Philips and Dutch IBM, and then an enquiry from NMB a major Dutch bank which resulted in a year's contract for three part-time people, Holland began to look like the most obvious market for them to move into full-time.

Tony knew it was a good target market, and set out to find a Dutch entrepreneur who could build the business from the firm base which had been created. To begin with Holland is only an hour away from Britain, and there has always been a strong affinity between the two countries in the service industries. The Dutch are very advanced in their technologies, and ready and willing to deal with English-speaking nationals. For several centuries the country's prosperity has been founded on the people's willingness to go out into the world and trade. They are open-minded and comfortable thinking on a large scale. Holland is an ideal country from which to launch an attack on Europe, being far less nationalistic than many of its neighbours.

Tony started working his traplines, asking all the people he knew in the country if they could recommend someone, trying to find the best salespeople working in the area. Cor Swart was at that time the marketing manager for ICL in Holland, his name was put forward and Tony was interested.

Cor is an entertaining Dutchman, with a flair for doing things with style. He lives in a small village south of Amsterdam. He started his career as an electronic engineer in the mid-1960s, working for Philips, and later for NOS which is Holland's national broadcasting corporation. While at NOS he became interested in the use of advanced switching gear, and that led to his developing an interest in the computing field generally.

He realized that if computing was what interested him, NOS was only on the fringes of the business, and that he needed to get inside a major bank or insurance company if he wanted to find out what was really happening. He settled on one of the latter, and stayed with them for two years, during which time his interest became aroused by systems building.

He moved on to ICL as a junior sales engineer, rising, in twelve and a half years, to be marketing director for the Dutch operation and systems and technical support manager. Following a merger with Singer, ICL had nearly 400 people working for them in Holland at that time.

Although he was not a consultant himself, Cor could see that that was where the future lay. He wasn't sure how to start about setting himself up in the business. One way would have been to join one of the big hardware companies, who were mostly entering the consultancy business, but he found that they were not able to afford the best consultants because of their rigid internal pay structures, and he wanted to work with the best. When he met Tony he realized that this was the opportunity he needed, giving him the chance to start from scratch in building the best consultancy in the business, with the best consultants in the marketplace.

Tony and his British team were over in Holland doing a presentation to a major client. They had already set up an 'operation' in Holland, which consisted of a mailbox in Amsterdam. They were intending to service the client from the UK if they won it, just as they did the others, and if they were not able to find the right person on the ground. A colleague of Cor's at ICL suggested that he should meet Tony, and Cor set out for the Marriott Hotel in the city centre, only to find that he was confronted by a team of five, instead of the one-to-one meeting he had expected.

Both Tony and Cor were impressed with one another, and both were keen to work together. A short mutual courtship came to an end at a two-day seminar, back at the Marriott, featuring Jim Martin. Susan, Tony's future wife, had gone over with a suitcase of envelopes to mail to prospective attendees of the seminar from the lobby of the hotel, and managed to bring in eighty people to hear Jim speak. Cor came to watch the show. He was convinced by Jim's performance that this was indeed the way the world was going, and signed up with Tony that evening.

Like all the founding entrepreneurs at JMA, Cor was a man who was willing to take a risk. Some years later he instigated the 20/20 Study, a project concerned with the future of telecommunications that was to grow quickly into a multi-million dollar operation worldwide. The business plan which he showed to Tony at the beginning made sense, and he was happy to set up with nothing more than the 50,000 guilders which Tony gave him as start-up money, plus the revenue from the contracts in Holland.

What had impressed Tony about Cor's business plan was that it had given a step-by-step account of how Cor would build the business and where he knew he would be able to recruit the consultants. Because ICL had had its own software department while he was working there he knew the market well, and all his predictions for the first eighteen months proved accurate. His numbers added up and he was in tune with the company philosophy of giving customer satisfaction and high levels of project management.

As with the other JMA starters, he woke up on 1 November 1982 with nothing, and had to go out and start a business himself, never having done anything like it before. On the first morning he went down to the village bookstore, which sold a few items of office stationery, and bought himself ten binders, so that he would be able to keep the company paperwork neat. By the afternoon he was wondering what to do next.

He very soon realized that he needed the stimulation of 'going to the office' rather than working from home. Offices, however, cost money. So it was with his courage in both hands that he approached the company which had been providing JMA with its mailbox service, and asked them to rent him some office space. He wanted to be in the centre of Amsterdam, so that he could concentrate on building the business away from the distractions of home and children.

They rented him the cellar of the building, which had such a low ceiling that Karel de Graaf, who at 6ft 5ins was the tallest of the consultants, had to walk about with a permanent stoop — a good incentive to keep out of the office and billing.

Not being a consultant himself, Cor could not bill himself out, as Tony had done, he was purely a manager and that meant he had to hire the best people in the business, quickly, and find work for them to do. Karel de Graaf came from Cor's ICL trapline, and Jan Blank, who had written a book on methodologies joined and later became managing director of Holland. Cor worked hard and immediately found good people. From the very beginning he set out to find someone to succeed him, so that he could go on to spread the business. After three or four hair-raising months the money started to filter in. During those months he had to learn the rules of cashflow, how to make it come in and stop it going out.

The company took root and grew at a spanking pace. Eighteen months later the Dutch team moved to 620 sq.m of office space slightly further from the centre — which was more space than the UK company had at that time. Within three years they had filled that and had rented two other offices alongside the original building. The consequent administration problems became ridiculous, and they started looking around for something more suitable.

Amstelveen is a suburb between Amsterdam and Schiphol Airport. It is a town in itself with its own mayor and city council and consists of a few office blocks, housing companies like KLM, the big banks and high-technology companies, and residential property. It is all set in parkland with wide open spaces and waterways. Cor decided that it would make the perfect setting for his growing operation.

The building which the company moved into was built at the end of 1987 by a celebrated modernist American architect. It consists of two three-storey wings and an enormous foyer area, sporting massive wall sculptures like the prow pieces from medieval ships. To help fill the wide open spaces of the foyer, Cor and his fellow tenants struck up a relationship with an art-gallery owner, who uses it as a display area.

The calm and peace of the surrounding suburb, deepens into a tranquil silence from behind the double glazing of this light, spacious building, the perfect atmosphere for a company of planners and thinkers.

Cor rented half of the block and let one of the floors out to KLM's data processing department, leaving himself with 2,100 sq.m of space. By the end of 1988 he was planning to take over the rest of the building within the next five years, giving himself a total of over 6,000 sq.m, to house the 250 people who he expected to be working there, compared with the seventy people there by the end of 1988. Throughout Europe by that time he had 130 people reporting to him.

To celebrate the opening of the new building, Cor invited Jim Martin over to give one of his lectures, as he was later to do in Ashford, and invited potential clients and other influential industry figures to listen.

From a standing start in November 1982, Cor was billing £8 million by 1989, and he saw no reason why he couldn't maintain that growth rate of over 50 per cent for the forseeable future.

In October 1989, 300 staff from JMA took over an ex-monastery hidden in the woods in northern Holland, for a 'JAM session', sleeping in the tiny rooms once inhabited by monks. James Martin, like a high priest, talked about the future, but by evening the tone was far from religious. All the nationalities of Europe danced to two bands until three and four in the morning. Jim danced with the secretaries and female information engineers. Each country put on a 'show'. They made Jim wear a Hamburg bargee shirt and scarf, and Shaun Boyle played a stand-up comedian. It seemed like the ideal way that European countries would work together after 1992. By Sunday everyone was ready to leave, tired and slightly amazed, feeling that they had been to a 'marvellous party'.

Initially the Dutch company was set up to handle the Benelux countries of Belgium, Holland and Luxembourg. Gradually it became obvious that Amsterdam was the ideal jumping-off point for the rest of Europe, and Cor found himself at the head of the European Division, with France, Germany and Switzerland falling under him. Most of the successful growth happened organically. Either Cor or Tony would win a slice of business in another city, such as Hamburg. In that case Cor sent Karel, who speaks fluent German, down to handle the job, he developed it well and had a business plan to take the company forward, and so JMA consequently found itself with a presence in Germany. A contract with BP in Antwerp and another in Brussels led to the recruitment of Vassily Kritis from Arthur Andersen, and suddenly they were active in Belgium. So that Vassily would have a P/L to manage, Cor and Tony gave him some business in Switzerland to handle. Vassily hired a manager to run Switzerland who didn't work out, proving to have the wrong philosophy.

The way that the network works is illustrated by the case of Banque Cantonale Vaudoise (BCV) in Switzerland. The initial enquiry from the bank came in to the UK office, but it was the Amsterdam team which actually followed it up.

BCV is among the largest cantonal banks of the Swiss Confederation with a reserve of 11bn Sfr. Cantonal banks are the state banks of Switzerland, and the BCV is one of the two cantonal banks of VAUD, one of the most beautiful cantons in the country, located on the north bank of Lake Geneva.

JMA was asked to perform an information strategy study during autumn 1986. In parallel BCV became the first bank worldwide to sign an early user contract for the IEF product (discussed in Chapter 13). A year after the first visit by JMA to Lausanne, BCV were performing three major infrastructure analysis projects (clients, securities and organization). By the end of 1987 four analysis projects had already been finished, one design and construction project was under way and at least five more design projects were starting up. Almost two-thirds of the data-processing human resources were committed to the JMA approach, with plans to increase the commitment the following year.

Early in 1987, BCV proposed to the two cantonal banks of Geneva a collaboration within the same framework and JMA assisted the Geneva banks to validate BCV's strategic models and the collaboration of the three became a fact. Information engineering had therefore established a common, standard environment for the development of information systems throughout the collaborative enterprise, and the JMA policy of growing accounts from the inside had paid dividends. With a client that large, it then becomes practical to start looking for other business in the same area, and setting up a permanent office.

Although most of their clients are international companies, requiring the same sort of service everywhere in the world, there are national differences which always have to be taken into account, and which require the expertise of local employees as well as international managers. In Portugal, for instance, there is a less sophisticated software industry, and it therefore takes longer for client companies to understand what it is that JMA is offering. As the technology builds up everywhere, however, the impetus to change and develop grows in strength, with waves of development happening simultaneously, and bringing less advanced countries forward at a much faster rate than their predecessors.

The culture of JMA says that if employees start as venture business managers, they can grow to become business centre managers. If they grow that large, they then have the opportunity to become business group managers and then business division managers. For someone with a clear idea of how to grow a business, and an ambition to achieve something quickly, there is nothing to stop them moving to the top at their own pace, taking on as much business as they can successfully handle.

Not every European start-up, however, went smoothly at the first attempt. At the same time as setting up in Holland, Tony also took 50 per cent in a Swedish company as he had in Italy with Lorenzo Bosio, trying all the same philosophies, but the relationship didn't work out and after nine months it was obvious that the two halves of the business were not heading in the same direction.

In France two more potential new managers did not work out and the company withdrew for a while, but now Cor's people are moving back into the market by servicing French clients from a French-speaking Belgian base.

With the approach of 1992, and the consequent creation, however gradual, of a united Europe, the selling opportunities for JMA are multiplied. When big companies start forming bonds across borders, they have greater needs for information handling systems, and they also have a greater capacity to pay for them. This binding together of different cultures means that all the major European companies are rethinking the way they do things, and they are being motivated to do things differently in the future. The magic data of 1992 is creating a momentum and getting big business to start up the processes of change. With the coinciding of the Olympics in Barcelona, the potential market for high-technology in Spain in particular is enormous, and they need all the help they can get from experts like the JMA team.

The internationalization of European companies is one of Jim Martin's favourite themes. He sites the success of Benetton, which has been largely due to the way in which they have used information technology to ensure that they get the right products to the right places at the right times. The company went from a standing start to having 6000 shops in 70 countries within just a few years.

The fashion industry is renowned for its toughness. It is a no-growth industry, with a complex structure of buying and stocking procedures. Benetton decided that they could only beat the established players in the market by using technology correctly. Whereas a buyer at Saks in New York is ordering clothes eight months before the store will be selling them, a Benetton manager is doing it two weeks before. The advantages of this speed of turnround in a business where a minute misjudgement of market tastes can spell ruin, are obvious.

Being an international company, Benetton needs to advertise all round the world, but a perceptive traveller will notice that the advertisements vary from area to area. This is because each market can react immediately to changes in buying patterns. If people are suddenly starting to buy green sweaters in New York their information systems will instantly inform them of this fact in Rome and green will be the colour they will be advertising in New York that week. If they are buying red in San Francisco they can change the ads in that area. It gives them total control over an operation which would otherwise have had its growth curtailed simply because of the cumbersome bureaucracy needed to support its size and rapid rate of growth.

There are many young, start-up companies in other industries which have pulled off similar coups against more established competitors who have been slower to accept the possibilities of technological tools. With the correct advice, many other companies operating in more than one country, Jim believes, can be as successful as Benetton.

The second area of triumph was Ireland, set up by Shaun Boyle. Shaun's success story is a perfect example of how the trapline theory worked. He was employed by Arthur Andersen as a consultant in Dublin, after working for them in both London and Brussels. Shaun, an archetypal Irishman who can do an excellent impression of a stand-up comic, had joined the giant multinational consultancy ten years before, straight from college. He was trained up in the mould of the 'big company man', but something deep inside him told him that this wasn't the right way for him to go.

He wasn't actively unhappy in his job, in fact he was very successful. It would not have been long before he became a partner, and Arthur Andersen are one of the most respected and established consulting firms in the world. It looked as if he was destined for a career as a successful company man. When he stopped to think about it, however, he couldn't help feeling that being a 'partner' in such a huge, amorphous company did not mean very much. It was really little more than a title, but he wasn't sure how else to approach his next career move.

A few years earlier he had heard about CACI from a colleague at Arthur Andersen who was auditing their books. He knew that there was an enormous potential in the database consultancy world, and that CACI had been reaping massive profits from their work in the sector. Although Arthur Andersen were heavily into the same field, Shaun did not feel that they had quite managed to find the right answers.

A colleague of his, whom he respected greatly, Ed Tozer, had already been recruited by Tony Carter for his newly set-up company in 1982, and Ed kept talking about how exciting the prospects for the company were. Like a true trapline victim, Shaun was intrigued, and when a meeting was suggested with Tony Carter he couldn't resist. He had taken the bait and just needed hauling in.

From talking to Ed he knew that Tony liked to find people with entrepreneurial spirit who wanted to set up and run their own shows. He decided that that was exactly what he wanted to do. He also believed that the product which JMA was selling answered all the problems which he thought Arthur Andersen was having with their systems. He could see that it was new, that it showed the user clearly how to utilize it, and he believed it was going to take the computing world by storm.

It sounded like an ideal opportunity for him and he prepared himself carefully for the meeting, writing a long and detailed business plan with which to impress Tony.

The meeting was arranged at the Sheraton Skyline, one of the more luxurious of the airport hotels at Heathrow. Thirty-year-old Shaun flew into Heathrow at tea-time, proudly clutching his lovingly prepared business plan.

Tony was like no one he had ever met before. Shaun was used to working with 'company men', people who talked business, business and then more business; people who worked by the book. At the Sheraton he was met by a jovial, enthusiastic man who seemed more interested in talking about Shaun's wife and four children than in the future of his business.

This was Shaun's introduction to a 'people interview'. One of Tony's main tenets is 'people buy from people'. He works on the theory that if he employs the right people, everything else will take shape around them. What Shaun didn't realize was that he was being assessed all the time. When he thought he was making small-talk, Tony was deciding whether he would 'buy from this man, work for this man, or want to socialize with this man'. Tony gave the business plan just the most cursory of glances, simply to satisfy himself that Shaun was a practical man who knew his business and had put some work into thinking about the situation.

In fact Tony had seen all he needed to see in Shaun's business plan with just a three-minute skim. He could see that it consisted of solid sales prospects, with people's names first and their company names second. He knew that this was the sign of someone who would be able to build something lasting. Anyone can name possible target companies, simply by consulting a directory, but to have named contacts in those companies who you know are ready to buy, puts the business on a completely different footing. Similarly, the plan contained a phased recruitment plan with identified names of the people who Shaun would be persuading to join him. These two simple ingredients, and attention to where the money would be coming from and going to, told Tony that they were on the same wavelength.

They spent the afternoon together by the Sheraton's exotic, tropical indoor swimming pool, had dinner in the hotel restaurant, and Shaun climbed back on the plane to Dublin that night feeling puzzled.

He knew that he liked Tony. He believed the product which he was selling was exciting, and he thought it would be very successful. He knew that he wanted to work for himself, and that it was the only way to achieve the sort of freedom which he wanted.

What he didn't know was why Tony had paid so little attention to his business plan. Did that mean that he didn't think it worth bothering with? Why hadn't they talked more about Shaun's experience, or about Tony's plans for the future? He couldn't make up his mind what exactly had taken place between them at the Sheraton.

Tony knew exactly what had taken place. He had found just the sort of man he was looking for. He usually had reservations about people who had worked for too long in big companies. They didn't always have the entrepreneurial spirit which he needed, although they often thought they did. He had already discovered that to his cost. He had wanted to get to know Shaun as a person, to assess whether they might be able to do business together. He believed that they could.

Neither of them had any illusions that Ireland was a small market when looked at globally, but with the right person it could grow to be a successful business centre just like any other. The work which Shaun could go after didn't have to be limited to Ireland. If he was the right person he would be able to grow a business anywhere. Tony needed people with the 'right stuff', if they could be found then nothing would stop the business from growing and prospering.

Tony was pretty sure that he had found someone with exactly the 'right stuff', and he moved Shaun up to the top of his trapline. He started bombarding him with material and writing him letters full of wild ideas and grand plans, anything to catch the young man's interest. Shaun was definitely interested. After a few months he realized that Tony was deadly serious in his offers.

After a couple more meetings they decided to go ahead. Tony offered to give Shaun £10,000 with which to set up the Irish office, and the most exciting few months of Shaun's life had started.

Suddenly the young executive who had never known what it was like to be on the outside of a big, paternalistic company, was out on his own. He had to find an office, he had to find office furniture, he had to win some business, he had to decide whether to hire a secretary, whether to buy a typewriter. From the biggest to the smallest he had to make endless decisions. If things went wrong he was going to have no one to blame but himself. It was a dizzying prospect, made all the more nerve-racking by the news that Ed Tozer, who had coaxed him into the company in the first place, had decided that he wasn't cut out to be one of Tony's entrepreneurs after all, and had gone to work as an independent consultant.

Shaun's wife Joan, who had always been supportive to his career, came in to help out with office hunting, typing and anything else she could fit in with looking after four children. They found a corner of a floor in someone else's office, and they found someone who was willing to take the risk of leasing them a computer.

While working out his notice at Arthur Andersen Shaun worked on his client trapline. He had rung round as many people as he could think of to tell them that he was going into business on his own, to explain the work which his new company was doing, and to find out if they had any jobs which they could put his way. Everyone was enthusiastic, everyone felt sure they would be able to talk business. He promised to ring back as soon as he was out of Arthur Andersen.

On his first day in business he rang everyone back, eager to get started on all the projects they had promised. As so often happens when you really need work, all the offers had suddenly become qualified. Jobs that looked as if they were going to be immediate suddenly weren't going to start for a couple of months, others were dependent on some future budgeting. His start-up money was slipping through his fingers. He still had his own mortgage to pay and family to feed, and he learnt the same hard lesson that Cor Swart and every other entrepreneur had to learn—the importance of cashflow. Unlike Cor, he did not have any existing clients or business on which to survive while he set the operation up.

Six weeks after the first frightening day Shaun did his first billable day's work, selling his services at £400 per day. The client was Frank Malin of the Electricity Supply Board, who had been the first named prospect in the business plan, and was later to join the Irish board of the company. Shaun had learnt, in those few exciting weeks, more about the laws of the business world than he had learnt in the previous ten years. He had been through a baptism in fire. By keeping his head and by continually working his traplines he managed to win a project in J. P. Morgan the merchant bank, which later led, via more traplines to another project on the Stock Exchange and another in Kleinwort Benson, and so the business grew. By finding out exactly who was responsible for signing the cheques, and asking them to pay within days, Shaun managed to get the cash in quickly enough to pay the bills. He never again had to ask Tony for money, or even ask his bank manager for an overdraft.

Shaun had been impressed by the company's connection with James Martin, a name he knew and respected, but it wasn't until he attended one of Jim's seminars and introduced himself, that they met for the first time. Shaun was actually able to introduce himself as the man who was setting up the Irish operation, and realized that although Jim was interested to hear what was going on, he was quite happy to leave the running of the business to Tony, and anyone whom Tony nominated.

Although he was having fun, enjoying the excitement and the danger, Shaun was also working long hours. Like Tony he had to worry about winning new business, setting up the physical side of the operation and actually doing the work himself. In many cases the only reason he won a tender for a job was because the clients knew that it was going to be him working on it. The next stage had to be to recruit a team to work with him if he was going to build a business centre as planned.

Working on the trapline theory again, he went back to his friends and colleagues at Arthur Andersen, and started talking to the ones whom he respected, and with whom he had enjoyed working. He worked on the same principles as Tony, drip-feeding them information, building up the workload and setting up contingency recruitment contracts with the right people.

Five years later the Irish office was fifteen-people strong, and handling big contracts both in Ireland and England. It had become a major part of the JMA empire, and Shaun had become group business development manager, overseeing the relationship with Texas Instruments (to be discussed in Chapter 13), and the group's expansion into new markets.

Now there were different problems for the managers of JMA. How could entrepreneurs like Tony and Shaun continue to attract other young entrepreneurs when they were starting to look like an established company? How could they persuade the people with the 'fire in their bellies' that JMA was still a young, dynamic and exciting company to work for? How can you stop a successful company from growing into exactly the sort of 'fat cat' which they had struggled to compete against at the beginning?

Although the company can now afford to put more money behind its entrepreneurs in new markets, there is a definite policy not to do so if it is possible to find someone who can 'bootstrap'. They actually need to find people who have the initiative and drive to set up operations from scratch, people who understand the importance of cashflow and the necessity of having the work before you hire the people. Without this solid grounding, new recruits to the cause cannot fully understand the philosophy of the company, they cannot become fully fledged members of 'the family'. Nor can the company hope to continue on its solid and steady path to growth if it is continually haemorrhaging money on new start-ups.

In the most difficult markets, such as France, it might be that the company would start to look at other methods of market entry, such as buying an existing company, but only once the options have been exhausted.

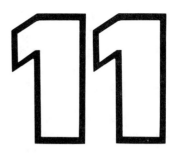

SHOOTOUT AT MOOSELIPS

- The founders begin to fall out.
- It is better to have an unhappy ending, than unhappiness without end.
- The right people to launch a new company aren't necessarily the right people to run a successful one.

By the end of 1982 Tony Carter's ambitions were steadily growing as the company became more successful. He began to assist DMW and DDI in their US business planning, and saw the potential to grow a worldwide group. Jim agreed that Tony should prepare a plan for such a project.

The plan was for rationalizing the American end of the fast growing multinational consultancy, and ironing out some of the conflicts of interest which Tony could see arising in 1983, particularly in the States.

There were talks going on with Texas Instruments at the time which were going to lead to massive opportunities and changes in direction for the company, and Tony wanted the organization to be in the right shape to take maximum advantage of the opportunities as they presented themselves. He wanted to change the management structure within the various companies, partly to consolidate his own powerbase, and partly to prepare them for the future.

His plan was that Jim and Dixon should remain as Chairmen of the company, while he became President. The corporation would consist of the Doll Martin Group Worldwide, under which umbrella would fall DMW Inc and DDI in the States, and DMW Europe (as it was still known at that stage). That would mean that the American companies which had previously been autonomous, would become answerable to him.

He flew out to Bermuda to meet Jim and Dixon and to put forward his ideas. Each of the companies, he explained, should continue to run with their existing managers, and after eighteen months they could review the performance of each of the sectors, splitting up the equity fairly according to results.

As usual Tony did a convincing selling job. Jim liked the idea but Dixon greeted it with a blustering hostility. Dixon was also a large man, like Tony, although he was built more along the lines of a truck than an athlete. In Dixon's mind Tony was a subordinate who needed to be reined in. Evenutally, however, he succumbed to Tony's arguments and Jim's reasoning.

Tony rented himself a house in Ann Arbor determined to move towards a new role as the head of an enlarged group, although by that time he was living mostly on aeroplanes and in airport lounges. He went to a group conference three weeks later to argue for the new arrangement.

In the end Jim agreed with Dixon that Tony was not the right man to run the whole operation, although he wasn't happy with Dixon's management style by then either. For the time being, however, the company would continue to be called DMW (Doll Martin Worldwide), and Tony would run Europe, not the USA. From then on Tony found Dixon increasingly belligerent whenever he confronted him. Dixon had particularly thick lips and Tony joked that they seemed to become larger and larger whenever he was arguing.

Don Brown, the then President of DDI was also at the meeting and Tony was told that Don would not agree to the plan. Not surprisingly Don took a dim view of having Tony brought in above him, where he had previously been in charge of his own show. Jim and Dixon did not want to upset Don and suggested the alternative of Tony looking after the consulting side and Don looking after the product side. Tony wasn't impressed, since he felt he was already doing just that. He insisted that Don Brown should be told that he would have to report to him, that he would be working *for* Tony, not *with* him. Don Brown refused to agree to this.

Don was a tall, elegant, very gentlemanly executive, always polite and humorous whatever the pressures. He resisted and disapproved of

Tony's aggressive style of takeover. Tony suspected that he could not build a strong products company. He began to formulate an alternative strategy and established an office in Reston, Virginia, in the suburbs of Washington, DC. There are now Silicon Valleys in many of the big cities of America such as Washington, Boston and Chicago, and they are the best places for consultants to set up shop. In Washington it is Reston which is the high-technology area.

Conflict with Don Brown wasn't the end of the problems for Tony. He found that he was becoming increasingly disillusioned with Dixon and the role he was playing in the group.

Dixon, in Tony's view, did not have the right personality to grow a large company. He was too tight-fisted. He did not reward his best people well and as a result they often left. He did not put enough money into product development. Worse, he seemed frightened to invest the sums needed to make new ventures grow. It was like gardening without fertilizer.

Tony flew out to see Jim again in Bermuda, and bared his soul. It was obvious that in the marketplace everyone now recognized the name of James Martin, but they were not usually aware of who Dixon was. There was little point in being linked to someone who did not help the cause in any way. Tony told Jim that the company he was setting up in America was going to be called James Martin Associates.

Dixon had not been forthcoming with his portion of the original start-up capital, and now the growing company was going to need much more financial backing, if it was to continue expanding. It was clear that the business needed to be fundamentally restructured. Tony went to the Bank of Bermuda to find out what money could be borrowed, using Jim's name. It was clear that a major confrontation was brewing.

Tony was determined to get his way. He knew that the developments between his people and Texas Instruments were going to be big, and he knew that they was going to lead to a conflict of interests on the product side. He stressed to Jim how hard he was finding it to work with Dixon and that, for his own peace of mind, he wanted just to be partners with Jim.

The main players came together for a series of meetings in Vermont. The mood was increasingly acrimonious. So much so that Jim encouraged Tony and Dixon to leave the house and discuss their differences one to one. They met up at Mooselips, a smoky bar with spit and sawdust on the floor; the sort of place where disputing rednecks break pool cues over one anothers' backs. The rowdy atmosphere suited Tony, but made Dixon, who was inappropriately dressed for such a venue, feel distinctly uneasy. The local woodchucks eyed him suspiciously, apparently hoping for an excuse to rough him up a little.

Eventually Martin agreed with Tony that the consulting company should be called James Martin Associates and should be run by Tony. Dixon was grossly insulted to think that they wanted to get rid of him and was determined not to sell out. The legal battle became bitter and prolonged.

At another meeting in Vermont, at a quaint little restaurant which advertised itself as 'Tucker Hill . . . warm and friendly with an altogether old fashioned essence', the battle raged on long after closing time. The chairs had been placed on the tables and a sad waiter sat in a corner until two in the morning, praying that the warring group would leave. Dr Carma McClure, a computer expert in the business was also in the party and became increasingly irritated. At a later meeting her patience finally broke and she dumped a glass of Perrier over Tony's head.

Dixon hired a lawyer who should have followed a career on the stage. His level of aggression and sense of drama worked to paralyse virtually every conversation. Tony later joked that if Dixon had chosen his consultants as well as he had chosen his lawyer, he would have had the most successful business in the world.

However formidable Dixon's lawyer was, he paled in comparison to Dixon's wife, who would attend the meetings personally if she felt some heavy artillery was needed. She had eyes which seemed to spray fear over the assembled company. Jim Martin had had to face both these fearful foes before, when he had tried to restructure the ownership of DDI.

Tony was determined to go ahead, however, whatever the opposition might do to him. He rechristened the company James Martin Associates, and announced that its territory was now worldwide.

JMA did not absorb DDI, which remained a separate company with Don Brown as the Chief Executive Officer. It was, however, desperately undercapitalized. In Martin's view it would have to have a large cash injection or it would die. Dixon refused to invest any more in it, so Martin eventually bought Dixon's shares, at a low price. He put money into the company and drove it to start developing the CASE toolset which he had been dreaming about.

Tony predicted that this would become a severe conflict of interest with JMA, and he was right. Martin thought that JMA would remain a consulting company at that time and DDI a software products company, but soon JMA was to have competing products.

DDI changed its name to KnowledgeWare, and grew vigorously. As small companies expand one of the most critical factors is having the right CEO. Sometimes a CEO who is good at the start-up phase is not so good for the growth phase. It eventually became clear to Martin that Don Brown, Dixon's appointee, could not grow the company as he wanted.

It is always unpleasant to fire somebody, especially when they are a charming person and a good friend. Martin bought Don Brown the best dinner he could find in Bermuda in the affluent old-world surroundings of Four Ways and, after the brandy, asked him to step down.

Don Brown was replaced by Terry McGowan, a quiet, tough ex-Vietnam helicopter pilot who proved to be an equally tough chief executive. KnowledgeWare eventually became a large software company, with no venture capital, and went public with a valuation of $134 million, reaching $150 million on the market two hours later. Ironically Don Brown was to end up a richer man than Tony because he kept his shares in KnowledgeWare.

Oddly enough, considering Jim's aversion to sport (he jokes that if he feels the urge for exercise coming on he goes to bed until it wears off), another great sportsman became the flamboyant CEO of KnowledgeWare—Fran Tarkington—one of America's most legendary football players. Terry McGowan was superbly effective as Tarkington's president.

At one stage Martin tried to merge KnowledgeWare and JMA. He felt that they needed each other, but it never worked out. Tony and Fran met to discuss the possibilities, but spent most of the day trying to outdo one another with stories of their sporting prowess.

The battle for JMA moved from Mooselips to the expensive offices of the aggressive corporate lawyer, goaded on by Dixon's wife. As KnowledgeWare grew rapidly it became clear that Dixon had made a mistake by selling his shares to Martin. He was determined not to make the same mistake with JMA. Eventually, however, Tony persuaded him to sell, and before long it was clear that he had repeated his error. Over the next five years JMA was to grow into a company which could have made Dixon rich beyond his wildest dreams.

It looked as if Tony was getting it all his own way, but he was still having terrible problems establishing the company in America, and in six years' time it would be him who would be negotiating how much money he would receive when stepping down as CEO.

12

AMERICA

- America is the biggest potential market for consultancy services in the world — it would be unthinkable not to be there.

- How not to do it.

- How to save the situation.

Some executives and sales people who can work wonders in the USA, find that in Europe their magic with people does not work. Similarly some Brits, as the Americans call them, can be great people-oriented executives in Europe but do not succeed in the States.

The USA was clearly the largest potential market for JMA, and right from his CACI days Tony Carter had been anxious to prove to the Americans that he could set up more successfully on their own soil than they could. He established an office near Washington, sent his son to college there, and set out to build an American JMA. All the costs of living accommodation and the setting up of the shell company, however, had to be passed back to the UK company. Although Tony won some American business, the company refused to take off like the British and Dutch operations.

Being stretched across the Atlantic proved too much for him to handle, so Tony recruited Chuck Lewis, who had been a senior vice president at CACI, to head up the US company. Martin was surprised at the choice, Chuck did not seem to him to have the same company-building spirit that Cor, Shaun or Tony himself had demonstrated in Europe; it seemed to colleagues that Tony was hiring Chuck simply because he was available, not because he was the right man for the job. He was fundamentally a technical manager with most of his experience in government work. He was not good at winning new clients.

Chuck won contracts, but never seemed able to build on these foundations and create a viable business. The company just did not seem to grow as it had in Europe.

It was a syndrome which Tony was to find occurring in several of the people whom he initially thought had the 'right stuff'. There is a big difference between having the ability to be a top consultant in a large organization where there is always someone else to talk over your problems with, and in actually closing sales and producing income from nothing. In Chuck's case Tony had made the mistake of recruiting him without getting him to prepare a business plan, as he normally would have done. Because there were some contracts to work on at the beginning, they were able to set up for business in some beautiful offices in Reston—not the sort of furnished accommodation which all the other country managers had started out in, and within three or four months Tony was beginning to feel uncomfortable about Chuck's lack of progress. It all went against the philosophy which he had been employing successfully in other parts of the group.

Tony decided that more needed to be done to get America going and he began to make a succession of judgements, not all of which were good. Another technician whom he knew and liked was Randall Rustin, a highly reputed database consultant who was running a small team of programmers from a fortieth-floor apartment in the heart of fashionable Manhattan. The office had a beautiful view but no profits. They were building personal computing software, something which had nothing to do with the work which JMA was doing. Randall was recruited by Chuck and his loss-making operation became part of JMA in America.

John King, the affable consultant who had worked with Tony on the BP job, was becoming disenchanted with Dixon Doll and Jim suggested that he set up a West Coast operation for JMA. John lived in Carmel in California and was allowed to operate from there. Carmel's main claims to fame are being one of the prettiest resort towns in the world and having Clint Eastwood as Mayor for a few years. It is not the sort of place which is conducive to hard work. It is also 3000 miles away from Washington. More losses began to pile up, which the UK company had to cover.

Around Christmas 1984, Tony, Chuck and Ian Palmer had a planning session at Martin's house in Bermuda. At 2.00 a.m. Martin walked Chuck back to his hotel across the Mid-Ocean golf course, letting Chuck dump all his feelings about the company to a background chorus of nocturnal insects. A sinking feeling grew in Martin's stomach that Chuck was not going to make it. He confided his fears to Ian the next day, and Ian agreed with them.

Chuck was not enjoying the work. When Tony flew into the States a few weeks later, and arrived in Chuck's kitchen, Chuck greeted him with 'You're going to fire me aren't you, well you're too late...' and handed him his resignation. He then went on to build a very successful career working within a large, secure company. Tony went out to Reston to take over JMA himself again, while trying to find someone else to replace Chuck.

John King went off to work as a freelance and Tony managed to minimize some of the losses by sending American consultants to work in other parts of the world, and cross-charging for them.

Because of Chuck's background the Reston consultancy was trying hard to win government work which is one of the hardest areas for any company to establish itself in. It takes years to build up the right degree of credibility, and until you do the only way to win business is to 'lowball', which means basically that you have to quote for business at prices which are so low that you can't possibly deliver anything worth having. JMA couldn't compete on price, since many of their competitors were using cheap labour like part-time housewives.

Tony stepped in and recruited two other managers who were equally ineffective at getting the business going and merely added to the outgoings. Unfortunately one of them became critically ill and could not work for about seven months. Later came Sean Yanosh. Sean was a colourful character, still in his twenties at the time. He was full of stories, which appealed to Tony, and anyone who heard all of them would have been surprised that he had managed to pack so much into such a short career—everything from brain surgery to working for the CIA in Afghanistan, from being smuggled into Tibet to setting up information systems single-handed for multinational companies. Sean did manage to bring in some business, including a contract with the Marine Corps, and some work with the Army which did not involve a contract since the instigator was trying to get things done without going through the contracting bureacracy of government agencies. It was better than nothing, but not enough to build a viable business.

Whatever Tony did right in Europe was not as effective in the States, and Tony worked out his frustrations in the normal manner, playing rugby, this time for the FBI. It began to look as if the company was not going to be able to build an American presence, at least not for the forseeable future. The problems were costing the rest of the company dearly and Tony knew that he was going to have to do something to stop the outflow of money, but he was very reluctant to give up his dream of establishing an American presence for the group.

He felt that he himself didn't have enough time to dedicate to the job, but he knew that it needed someone senior and experienced to pull it off. The directors could see from the figures that something needed to be done if the American end of the operation wasn't to bring down the whole group, and Ian Palmer was suggested for the job.

Ian does not fit the popular image of an American CEO. A New Zealand version of Woody Allen, he is often gloomy, with an acerbic wit and long, wild hair. He is meticulous, nit-picking, more like a lawyer than a salesman, but his logical mind and technical skills were largely responsible for the focus and success of the British company and for the creation of the methodology. He was also surprisingly successful as a salesman and manager. There are many sales courses which describe any number of different ways of closing a sale. Ian had a technique all of his own, which Tony described as the 'end-of-the-world close'. He would basically describe to the prospect how doom would strike, leaving his business in ruins, if Ian's methods were not adopted. Certainly he was nothing like any of Tony's other country executives, and the idea of setting him loose in America caused Tony some concern, possibly because he didn't like the idea of Ian taking on something which he had started and radically changing its style.

At that stage the US company needed someone who could not only handle the business which existed, but could build it up into something more lasting and worth while. Tony himself had serious doubts as to whether the professorial Ian would be capable of such a task. Other members of the board believed he could, and persuaded Tony to give him a try. It was to prove a sound decision and Tony later acknowledged that Ian did a very good job.

Sean Yanosh was still there, and bitterly resented having Ian brought in over his head. Six weeks after Ian arrived Tony called him and Sean back to the UK to talk it over. They left knowing that Ian was in charge and that Sean would be assessed over the next eighteen months to see if he should be Ian's successor when he returned to the UK as technical director. The situation conflicted with Tony's gut feeling at the time, that Sean was better for the job of growing the company in the aggressive US market, and put another wedge between Tony and Ian.

Initially Ian Palmer agreed to go across to America for two years to get JMA's US operation up and running. He said he would set the company on its way and then come back to Europe. He bought an attractive house in Vienna and moved his family over to join him. In the end he found it harder to tear himself away then he had imagined.

He was not taking over much of an operation at that time. There were three consultants working in the Reston office, all of whom needed education in the concepts of information engineering. There were two clients, both sections of the armed forces; one with no contract. A sustained plan was now needed for winning new business. The existing base of business was running at a profit but with only six months' work ahead.

Given the degree of chaos and the lack of management which he found there, it was not hard for Ian to find ways of improving the operation. his first priority was to look for more revenue from the few clients which the company had, such as the US Marines. The thought of Ian Palmer selling to the US Marines seemed improbable, but somehow he managed to hypnotize them with his finely detailed descriptions of how information engineering would help them, and he began to grow their operation.

He then set out in search of new customers. It was a familiar JMA situation. Ian was starting almost from scratch, just like Cor Swart in Holland. Because of their work in Europe, and because of Jim Martin's backing, JMA were the leaders in their field. The problem in America was that no one knew who they were. It was largely a question of marketing.

He had to start simultaneously recruiting and selling hard, while making the books balance at the same time. He was determined to vastly raise the standards of recruiting and not to have to ask the European end of the group for any more money, working instead on the tried and tested JMA method of pulling a company up by the bootstraps, which might slow progress down, but at least ensures that anything which is built is on firm ground. He continued to work the recruitment traplines, but he became far more selective and rigorous in his choices. He found that the best hunting grounds were the consultancies which were doing a lot of work for the government, as CACI had been. Most of these companies had ferocious 'hire-and-fire' policies of management, and consultants working within them found it hard to produce worthwhile project results because of the bureacracy of all government agencies. These people were mostly keen to move to a company which seemed to be doing exciting work on the leading edge.

Once recruited the consultants had to be trained in the world of information engineering, but Ian couldn't afford to have them in classrooms for two months, being taught by people who were also needed out in the field producing revenue. He had to design a self-training system, consisting of examples of project deliverables from the UK to demonstrate what was being done, and the studying of all Jim's books and videos and the methodology handbooks. By the time the consultants reached the clients they knew more about information engineering than any competitors.

Ian is a classic workaholic, often staying at his screen until late into the night. His hard work is always highly focused and meticulously detailed; the business began to come under control. He soon realized that winning government business was the hard way to grow, and he started planning to win clients in the commercial arena.

The methods which had built the European success story finally started to take root in Reston under his guidance. By the end of the first year he had fifteen people on the payroll, a year later he had doubled that number to thirty, and a year later it was up to 60 and by 1989 it was over 100, with all of them fully employed and the money rolling in.

While undertaking this recruitment campaign he was constantly aware that, although he did not leave after two years as originally planned, he still needed to recruit his own successor if the company was to continue to grow to its full potential in the States once he had moved on. This was the point at which things had gone wrong before. The problem was in finding someone who had the right balance of experience and ambition to want to take on a still relatively unknown consultancy, and turn it into something major.

Because the Dutch and Irish operations had been so successful under the leadership of people who were natives of their own territories, Tony felt that JMA needed an American national to handle the American operation on an ongoing basis. In fact there were many examples of non-nationals successfully running national operations. Belgium was managed by a Greek, Germany by a Dutchman. There were also some failures managed by nationals including France, Sweden, Australia and Singapore.

One of Ian's first US recruits was Gary Yates, who played volleyball for relaxation with an expatriot Australian called John Wyatt. Before long John was being seduced by the JMA trapline method of recruitment.

John had trained in Sydney with Arthur Andersen. After a brief stay at Chattanooga in Tennessee, working on a contract for Andersens, John had fallen in love with America. Deciding to make a more permanent move he had joined Touche Ross in Washington. He worked there as a manager for a time, enjoying the flexibility of the company's approach, but eventually becoming frustrated by its lack of growth. Like Shaun

Boyle and the others, he felt an urge to try his hand as an entrepreneur and went into business with a like-minded partner.

The personal computer boom was by then in full swing, so the two of them set up a company consisting of two retail outlets, working along the lines of Computerland, backed by a consultancy business providing 'turnkey' PC operations for companies such as real estate agencies and law practices.

The company was reasonably successful, despite the tight profit margins which exist in the microcomputing business. When the partners sold out, after installing over 300 systems for clients, the company was turning over around £3 million a year, and they had gained some invaluable experience in the problems of setting up and running their own operation.

John was then unsure of what his next move should be. Although the selling of the business meant he now had some capital, it certainly wasn't enough to live on, and he wanted to work anyway. His friend Gary Yates suggested that JMA might be an interesting next move for him, and arranged a meeting with Ian Palmer. The trapline was gently hauling in another good catch.

John remembers his initial impression of Ian as a typical Englishman in the colonies who looked as if he should have been wearing a pith helmet. Ian struck him as something of a nutty professor, quirkish but with very clear and resolute objectives. Ian was immediately impressed with John, feeling sure that he had found the right man. He made him an offer, and John went back to Australia for a couple of months of rest and relaxation while he thought over what he wanted to do next with his life.

As he travelled around his homeland, from Brisbane down to Adelaide, visiting friends and relations he hadn't seen since moving to America, he weighed up the options before him. Ian's offer was very tempting. Working with JMA would provide him with the right mix of management, marketing and consultancy work. It was a company which seemed to be gaining a solid foothold in the States, but one which had a long way to go. He decided to accept the offer.

When John joined the company it had about a dozen consultants. He brought an additional trapline, contributing to the search for the best people JMA could find in the business. It is always hard to find consultants and managers of the right calibre for the sort of work which JMA undertakes. A consultant who can work for, say, a telecommunications company which is changing its entire business every two or three years is very different to the sort of person used to working in a more staid environment such as banking, where the majority of consultancy experience has been gathered in the last decade.

Typically the people JMA are looking for are in their mid-twenties and have moved around a bit already, either in other consultancies or in client companies. That way they are more likely to know what they want from a job, and to be ready to settle down and stay in one place for a few years, or preferably for an entire career. That makes them expensive. An average JMA consultant in the US was being billed out at $1,200 a day by 1989, and many for as much as $1,500.

As he worked more closely with Ian, John found his opinion of him changing. He found that the 'nutty professor' facade actually covered an able manager who made good recruitment decisions and was skilled at matching the right people to the right jobs. He soon discovered, however, that Ian was not a 'people person', being too inclined to be blunt and undiplomatic at times when people didn't necessarily want to hear the whole truth. Clients either loved him or hated him. He was always very honest, clear and rational in his analysis of situations. He had a strong reputation within the industry for his work, and he was building an able team of managers who knew how to handle clients with kid gloves. As a unit they began to fire up.

John's first job was to take over JMA's relationship with Amoco, the American oil giant, based in Chicago. It involved him in a lot of travel, but he didn't mind at that stage. He liked the city, and he could see that there was potential growth for JMA within the client. Amoco were working on a number of projects at the time, doing business area analysis projects to improve their ability to build, plan, schedule and control their oil refining and distribution activities across the country. With greater control they believed they could make far more money. They just needed to be given the right techniques. After a year on the job himself, John hired a manager and built up a team of six permanent people in Chicago.

As the practice in Washington grew, jobs started to come in from other parts of the country and several strong client bases began to become apparent in other cities. Ian did not particularly subscribe to Tony's Country Manager is King philosophy, but parts of it became useful. Since they had to look outside Washington for non-government work, it was inevitable that they would need other 'business centres'. As a client grew large enough they would start to recruit people locally to handle the business. Once they had recruited enough people to justify it they would then open a local office, which would have a manager who reported back to Reston. Ian was keen not to build up 'territories' as was happening in Europe, since he believed that the secret of growth lay in synergy and free exchange of people and experience.

Firstly the Amoco work required a sufficiently large local JMA team for it to be worth while opening an office in Chicago and going after more local business. Work for Xerox in New York made it worth opening up for business in New Jersey, and a contract with Imperial Oil led to an office opening in Toronto.

There were a number of ways in which Ian and John set about winning new business. The project which JMA was working on with Texas Instruments was beginning to be sold into companies on a Betatest basis, and many of the customers needed consultancy help with learning how to use the software. So the JMA consultants started to follow the TI sales team around the country. They also tried to link in with KnowledgeWare sales people wherever possible. Another source of contacts were the James Martin Seminars. At that time Jim was holding eight a year in the States, attracting around 250 people to each. This meant a large 'captive' audience of Martin fans, who would be hearing him speak about information engineering as part of the seminar. The JMA team would set up a hospitality suite in the same hotels and get to know as many managers as possible.

Ian also arranged an Information Engineering Forum in Chicago, a conference at which people who were already doing it would talk about their experiences to those who were potential clients. Attendees had to pay for their seats, which meant more revenue for JMA.

It soon became apparent to Ian that John would make the ideal successor. He had the entrepreneurial and marketing experience, as well as being a bright consultant. They had to convince Tony, who had set his heart on having an American national in the job. Other candidates were put forward for consideration, but in the end Tony agreed that John was the best man for the position. He asked Ian, however, to stay in America another year, to keep an eye on the way the business was developing.

Whereas JMA had been handling almost exclusively government work when Ian came out from Britain, the balance had changed during his stewardship, and they were handling at least 80 per cent commercial work by the time John had been running the office for a year. Although business was going well, it was still something of a pioneering situation. Few people outside their existing client base had heard of JMA in America, and use of methodologies generally is not as advanced in the States as it is in Europe, where companies are more aware of the need to use technology to get the best out of their people.

Ian and John have very clear ideas on how to create a consultancy operation that will grow. They believe that it is vital to have a single culture and purpose. In the case of JMA that purpose is built around methodology, and everything works from that basis. Many other consultancies work on the premise of having teams of very good people working very hard to solve whatever problems the client has in whatever way they can. While that can lead to a successful day-to-day business, John firmly believes that it does not lead to long-term growth.

Jim's books and videos play a vital part in the creation of the company's culture, and act as a shop window for their services. Customers can read Jim's books and understand the importance of what he is teaching and how it will effect their businesses. The books do not, however, give the readers enough detail to be able to go away and do the work. For that they need help, and that is when they will turn to JMA.

Being something of a pioneering operation, there is a spirit of excitement and adventure about JMA. It is not unlike the spirit which pervaded the early computer companies of California, like Apple. Technical people come to work for JMA, and stay with them, because they are the ones who built the systems in the first place and they enjoy working with the methodologies and getting to play, improve, experiment and argue about their pet subjects with like-minded people. With a team that enthusiastic it is impossible for a company not to grow fast.

John and Ian see no reason why the American operation shouldn't grow quickly to 400 or even 500 people, selling consultancy services, seminars, training, books and other products. John has now settled himself in Reston, and bought a five-acre farm, which he is setting about renovating. In 1989 he and Ian had ten managers out consulting and helping to build the company. A sales team is also being created and direct-mail and telemarketing campaigns are being planned for selling 'packaged expertise' (discussed in more detail later). The American arm of the company was well and truly up and running.

While Tony couldn't deny Ian's success at turning round the American operation he felt increasingly uneasy with Ian's style of management and presentation. The split between Tony and Ian was becoming increasingly obvious to the other directors. Equally Ian felt that Tony's management style was becoming incompatible with the way the company was going, and was in fact holding it back, and made his views well known.

TEXAS INSTRUMENTS AND THE IEF

GETTING INTO BED WITH A GIANT

- The relationship with Texas Instruments.
- Taking the business a quantum leap forward.
- A giant company can provide the resources to turn the ideas of a small company into reality.
- A consultancy can sometimes sell products too.

At the conference in Ann Arbor where Tony was to be made president of the corporation, Jim mentioned that he had had meetings with some senior people at Texas Instruments (TI). He suggested that Tony should get in contact with them since they were in need of having some methodology written. Taking this sort of lead and building it into a piece of business was exactly the way that Tony liked to work. At that stage, however, he could have no idea of just what a massive piece of business it was going to turn into.

Some months before senior executives within TI had decided that they needed to rethink how they developed computer systems. They believed that they particularly needed to improve their productivity and the flow of vital information through the company.

Jim had worked with Texas Instruments for some time and found the company exciting. He regarded their information systems executive, John White, as one of the best and most innovative in the world.

A couple of years before, the TI chairman Mark Shepherd, and president Fred Bucy had flown down to Bermuda (in two TI jets — one each), to spend a week consulting with Jim.

At the request of TI's top management, John White and two other IS managers flew north from the heat of Dallas to talk to Jim in the clear air of the Sugarbush Inn resort in Vermont. The meeting lasted for three days. On the first day the men from TI outlined their plans, the progress they had made so far and the problems which they were facing. Jim just listened, giving his feedback on the second day, which led the small group on to general discussions on the third day about the way a company should be going when it has reached the size and power of TI, and how they should be preparing for the future.

TI had all the classic problems which JMA had been addressing on behalf of all their clients. As in most large commercial companies, their computer systems were taking too long to deliver, when they delivered they were not satisfying expectations, meaning that they had to be changed, which was a difficult thing to do and required an enormous amount of effort from large numbers of people (about 2000 of them worldwide at TI). Worst of all there is a great shortage of skills to do all this work. Through information engineering, Jim and JMA were addressing themselves to the task of putting systems engineering to develop commercial data processing systems on a similar basis to other engineering disciplines.

After three days the TI executives left Vermont with their appetites whetted, they felt they had come upon the right man and the right ideas. Everything he had said had confirmed the thoughts which had already been taking root within the company. They felt that all the ideas were on the right track, they just needed to find a way of implementing them.

Tony was more than just interested in the tip-off. TI is one of the giants of the high-technology field, a world leader in microchips, and a manufacturer of defence equipment, computers and consumer products, with annual sales of $5 billion. It is a company which is respected in the industry for its research and development work, seeming to be driven by engineers rather than marketing people, as happens in most of the big high-technology companies. It seemed like the perfect type of client for JMA, a company with massive marketplace brawn, in need of some help from outside brains, but at that stage it did not seem an obvious 'business partner'.

Ian telephoned Dallas to introduce himself and made contact with Stu Bunday who was to be in charge of the project. The TI management felt that they were on the right wavelength and sent some people over to London to talk face-to-face with JMA's people and decide if the hunch was worth following up. The TI people stayed in the stately Hyde Park Hotel, one of the elegant establishments dividing Knightsbridge from the Park, and they met Tony and Ian Palmer for lunch at Mr Chow's, the fashionable Knightsbridge restaurant frequented by denizens of the fashion, showbusiness and business worlds.

The TI executives asked whether the JMA team, if given the contract, would be willing to go down to Dallas to critique their current systems development methodology, and make some recommendations. The answer was an unequivocal 'yes'. The TI executives did not give an immediate decision, but went off to Germany on other business to consider the situation. On the following Thursday, when the Americans returned to London, JMA had prepared some recommendations and a letter of contract. On the Friday the letter was signed. The speed of the agreement was almost unprecedented for such a large company. The fee was to be $40,000. At that stage there was still no indication of just what the project would grow into.

Ian Palmer headed out to Dallas for two weeks to see what was wrong with their set-up. He talked to a variety of systems development people and end users, finding out what they were doing and reading their documentation. Tony flew out once the study was done and the two of them then put their heads together back at their hotel to create a presentation, recommending what TI should do to improve things.

That could have been the end of the job for JMA, but both they and TI were simultaneously beginning to think along broader lines. As a first step, however, the JMA team wanted to win the job of putting into practice all the recommendations which they had made.

TI is a huge corporation. At one time it dominated the northern area of Dallas, and it still has around half a dozen major office complexes within the suburb of Plano. Dallas was booming at the time, with new buildings springing up between every visit.

The style of the TI buildings is always the same, like a cross-fertilization between a science park and a university. They are single-storey buildings, with open-plan offices giving off a quiet, efficient air. The main compound is dominated by a giant earth satellite dish. Although the people are typical Texans in their informality, security is rigid; silent cameras follow everyone wherever they go, and a visitor isn't even allowed to go to the bathroom without a chaperone. Their company philosophies are very different from JMA's. TI is a huge bureaucracy, a multinational giant, but its heart is set in 'Middle America'.

When JMA technicians first arrived, they were amazed to walk into reception and see a security guard, with his cowboy-booted feet up on the desk, holstered gun and ornate belt buckle on his Levis. It was a culture shock after the formal and discreet style of companies like IBM. The cowboy style was evident everywhere, with as many pick-up trucks parked in the company car park as saloons. Many of the managers would wear boots (shit-kickers as they referred to them) under their business suits. Different as they were, however, the two companies were soon to find that by working together they could achieve a quantum leap in the world of technology. Tony felt very comfortable among the fun-loving, hard-drinking Texans, being the life and soul at parties and in restaurants. The Texans, in return, seemed to admire his entrepreneurial skills.

The initial recommendations which Ian Palmer had made were well received, basically because the TI management had already decided that that was the way they should be going, and had been looking for an objective confirmation from JMA. They had already decided to create the post of information centre manager, to set up an Advanced Technology Centre, and to start using fourth-generation languages.

After the presentation John White, TI's information systems manager took Tony into his office and asked him what he thought they should do about their problems. Tony told him that he thought the best bet was information engineering, and suggested that JMA should put together a proposal for handling the work for them. John White agreed and Tony and Ian returned to England to work on it.

A few weeks later Tony was back in Dallas with the proposal. He now knew that he was on the verge of landing a very big contract. The adrenalin was racing. Both he and Phil Passmore, who was the Manager of the Advanced Technology Centre, were planning to fly down to Ann Arbor to attend one of Jim's conferences. On the plane going down, as they both relaxed with their in-flight drinks, Phil asked Tony how much it was going to cost to employ JMA to implement the proposals. The answer was $1 million. Phil managed not to spill his drink and, after an initial intake of breath, he agreed, although the final contract took eight months to draw up. It was a tremendous coup for such a new and small consultancy to be given such a mammoth job by such an established company.

The subsequent business with TI led to JMA's winning the Queen's Award for Export in 1986, and this was still only the beginning of the relationship.

Even before the contract was signed, between five and seven JMA people were working permanently on the writing of the methodology. TI rented houses and apartments for everyone who was going to be there for more than a few weeks.

Phil Passmore remained a dedicated champion of all Jim's ideas, and ran his department in an autocratic and dictatorial style. Many of the consultants found the style hard to work with, but it had the advantage of shielding them from the political battles which were going on among the top managers as to what to do with the product which they were creating. Consultants like Keith Short, who had been working on similar projects at CACI, were recruited and became excited at the prospect of finally seeing the ideas they had been working on for years come to fruition. In the end some of them were to stay out in Dallas for two years, but no one knew that at the beginning. Like most consultants they were hired for three months to start with, and then they were given one- or two-month extensions as they went along. It was not a stable atmosphere to work in, but it was a stimulating one and many of them believe that without Phil's dedication to the project they would never have reached a successful conclusion.

Everyone on the team was excited by the potential of what they were doing, and people began to talk about the possibilities of automating the methodology. It was an idea which Jim had been thinking about for some time, and prototypes had been built in the past. He had just needed the right partner to work with. Tony was excited by the idea, but knew that the amount of money that would be needed to invest in the work was way beyond the capabilities of JMA. The people at TI had also been considering the possibilities of creating a product which they could sell to the outside world. About three weeks into the work Tony asked Phil what he thought about the possibilities of automation. Once the subject was out in the open, and the possibilities there for all to see, discussions began in earnest.

TI became fired up about the project work which was under way, and there was a fierce team spirit among everyone on the team. They set up an artificial intelligence machine at Jim's house in Bermuda a year later, and sent up a team of programmers and architects to work with it. TI rented a house nearby for Bob Bates and a large cast of itinerant analysts to live in, and it seemed that money was no object. A project which had started out as an exercise in putting their own house in order, now looked as if it might have massive global commercial possibilities.

TI had been looking for software tools that could match their own in-house needs for some time. They had found several possible products, but they were very isolated and did not cover the entire development life-cycle. They really wanted to automate the entire development process. They had found the way with Jim Martin's methodology, as practised by JMA and what had happened as a result of the initial three-day meeting with Jim Martin was that TI had changed the way it developed applications and ran its IS organization.

It changed the IS relationship with end-users. TI went ahead to establish information centre operations which served end-users with spectacular success on a worldwide basis, and TI measured the many millions of dollars a year which this added to their profits. If the idea had worked so well on their own problems, and they could package the answers up automatically, why would they not work as well for other people? It suddenly seemed the obvious way forward for the industry, fitting in with everything which Jim Martin believed in and preached.

In the end TI was to invest many millions of dollars into developing the information engineering facility (IEF) product. JMA were the architects providing the plans, but it was TI who actually built the walls and owned the resulting house. The architects, however, didn't intend to let their role stop there. Tony wanted to be part of the sales bonanza which he and Jim were confident would happen when the product became available to the world's markets.

Although this is not intended to be a technical book, it might help to explain in a little more detail what this development actually means, starting with the methodology upon which everything else is based. The term information engineering, which Jim Martin invented and spread throughout the industry, sums up exactly what the methodology achieves. The word 'engineering' is used to imply that the methodologies involved use formal disciplines with precise, well thought-out techniques, rather than the 'making it up as you go along' techniques of traditional programming, from the pioneering days of software design.

Information engineering therefore refers to the set of interrelated disciplines which are needed to build a computerized enterprise based on data systems. It focuses primarily on the data which is stored and maintained by computers and the information that is distilled from this data.

If a corporation has a good information system, information engineering can formalize the techniques by which the systems are created, using different types of diagrams, tools and methods from those used by software engineering. Once it has been formalized it means that computers can be programmed by computers, cutting out the time and money wasting stage of employing human programmers.

The basic premise of data processing put forward by Jim is glaringly simple. It takes as a starting point the premise that data lies at the centre of modern data processing, and that creating and modifying that data requires appropriate accuracy controls. Processes can then handle virtually every informational requirement for the company, printing routine documents such as invoices, receipts, freight bills and work tickets, creating summaries or analyses of the data. Charts and reports can be produced, and vital 'what-if' questions can be asked and answered, giving managers the power to see everything that is possible in the future, and to make more informed decisions on how to proceed in every area of the business.

The idea of the IEF product created by TI and JMA was to create a software package, which would sell at around $300,000 a time, and which would help client companies to bridge the gap between their computer facilities as they are now and as they ought to be in the future.

At the heart of IEF is the central encyclopaedia that holds all the types of information about the business, the processes and the functions within a company's activities. That links with a local encyclopaedia into which details of the company's operating needs are fed. That in turn is tied to various 'toolsets' through an intelligent workstation that can handle advanced graphics.

The five toolsets are: planning, which is used to devise an information strategy that suits the business; analysis, which focuses the managers' minds on putting correctly all details of their company's business into the model; design, which creates solutions to the 'problems'; code generation, which produces the programmes to realize the chosen solution, and database generation which creates the information structure that will run the system when it is finally commissioned.

One of the most important selling points for CASE systems in general, however, is that they give a computerized business the chance to eliminate almost all the very high costs of maintaining the software— which might account for anything up to 70 per cent of data processing budgets in most companies. Without IEF the gap is bridged laboriously by hundreds of programmers and analysts producing charts following the tedious progress of endless invoices, on which plans for the future can be based. Skilled staff are expensive and in short supply, which means the processes become slowed down and the results are often obsolete before they have even been produced. The IEF package would be a giant leap into the future, automating all stages in the design and development of new computer systems.

A machine code that tells a computer what to do can take a roomful of programmers months to specify and design, let alone the trial runs needed to eliminate all errors or bugs. The final software product will be capable of handling many different interlocking tasks, and any error in the instructions for one might influence its ability to perform many others. It has to be better to automate.

Architecture, the combination of intuitive design and rigorous discipline, is as important to the development of information systems as it is to the building of high-rise office blocks. If a company gets it wrong at the design stage nothing will rise higher than ground level, let alone fulfil a worthwhile role. Anything that does get built to faulty specifications is likely to fall down later or, at best, require constant expensive maintenance work.

Information engineering brings the disciplines inherent within civil or mechanical engineering to the development of information systems. The concept calls for the information systems development process to be covered, step-by-step, from information strategy planning, through the analysis of information needs and the definition of the required information system, to the construction of operational systems and their implementation. This entire procedure is covered by the information engineering methodology (IEM).

The automation of information systems is controlled over seven identifiable phases. The final phase generates the various applications from the analysis and specification work undertaken during the previous phases. The net result of what is a detailed and thorough interaction with the end-user, is a coherent information system that is user-friendly, flexible and future-proof. The main characteristics of this system are the common use of data, the accessibility of data and interconnectivity.

The IEM uses the objectives of the enterprise's business plan as its foundation. The information is provided at all levels within the enterprise and is therefore geared to the requirements of the user, and not to incidental technical circumstances or the vagaries of traditional development techniques.

So rigorous and detailed is the approach taken by the IEM, that it can only be fully implemented with the aid of computer-based tools.

A logical consequence of information engineering is the identification of highly sophisticated, pan-enterprise systems, integrated within the fundamental information systems strategy.

To build such systems, and maintain enterprise-wide process and data integrity, demands the support of a powerful and sophisticated software system. This is where IEF comes in, automating the processes of IEM.

The IEF is far more than a personal productivity tool for the systems analyst or designer. It is a complete, automated information systems life-cycle support environment, that offers as much to operational systems maintenance as it does to information strategy planning.

It is applicable to many different industries and organizations, but due to its scale and implementation, it is primarily targeted to support IT development in highly complex, multi-system organizations.

In use it enhances the benefits of the methodology still further, providing a significant improvement in productivity in the support of the complete information systems life-cycle. It enables corporations with significant applications backlogs to catch up.

The development of new computer applications using conventional techniques is both labour-intensive and time-consuming, and therefore expensive. The IEF offers the potential to reduce systems development timescales by between 20 per cent and 80 per cent.

The basic idea is simple. As with other labour-intensive operations, individual tasks of the systems development specialist can be translated in procedures that, in turn, can be automated. These functions are then executed by computers with their proven ability to process huge volumes of data, very quickly and with unwavering precision.

Information engineering and the IEF actively promote the users input to, and access to, information systems. Using these tools, new systems are developed that genuinely meet the needs and demands of the user community. Both IEM and IEF therefore represent a challenge to most corporations and call for a new generation of information systems specialists to work in an environment where IT and the core business are as one.

The managers at JMA realized that if the IEF package could be sold commercially, customers would need advice and training on how to install and operate it. On the back of the product package JMA would therefore be able to sell consultancy services, perhaps earning two or three times the cost of the initial package as a result. Under the guidance of a JMA consultant, the client simply has to enter his requirements on a screen; colourful diagrams then replace acres of paper, and an outline of the new system resolves itself before their eyes. Then a button is pressed and the required programming takes place automatically, rendering the programmer redundant.

The system is designed so that it can be updated in future with the minimum of fuss. It incorporates an 'encyclopedia' of information detailing an organization's every computing need—a central repository of rules and information—which JMA strives to keep aligned with business objectives.

The potential for the market seemed good. When the top brass from
TI gathered around the machine for a demonstration of what IEF could
do, they immediately decided to go ahead with the project, issuing
instructions to build it and exploit it commercially. The JMA team were
more than keen to go out and market the product on TI's behalf.

Rank Xerox was one of the early buyers for the system. At their
international headquarters, information management staff supported by
JMA consultants were able to tackle the analysis of a complex business
area spanning RX activities across the world. The resulting business
system design projects will use the PC and mainframe components of
the IEF to generate systems which embody the company's corporate
commitment to quality throughout the commercial operations.

By using IEF during 1987, RX(UK) were able to generate a business
systems development programme building on the work they had already
completed in defining the roles, responsibilities and objectives of the
organization, and the gaps and mismatches within their existing systems.

In common with the US-based Xerox corporation, RX had high
expectations of accruing productivity gains which would enable these
systems to be ready for implementation far more quickly than would
be the case using traditional methods. However, for RX, quality of
specification was the most important objective, and productivity gains
were the 'icing on the cake'.

When Rolls-Royce bought the IEF, the total package including
consultancy was worth nearly £2 million.

At Volvo Data AB, the Volvo owned computer services bureau, IEF
has led to substantial savings in project development time. Their first
production project, despite the learning curve and using beta-test
software, halved the time it would have taken to develop with traditional
methods, cutting costs by £200,000. The total programming development
time in a traditional environment would have been about 169 employee
weeks. Analysis and design stages would have brought the total to 270
employee weeks for the whole project. The first project was a medium
sized application for budget control, which would normally have been
done by about three analysts and seven or eight programmers. With
IEF they used only two analysts and all the COBOL and SQL code was
generated automatically without programmers.

Volvo Data AB also markets its services to other commercial
organizations and the IEF gave it a useful competitive edge in developing
systems for new customers and services. Volvo went on to start five
other projects on the IEF, including a sales and accounting system.

The result at Volvo is a 'cultural revolution', with hundreds of programmers now being retrained for analyst and designer jobs.

The first client to demonstrate the full ability of IEF was Nykredit, a bank in Denmark. When changes in Danish law made foreign currency loans available to Danish citizens, the bank wanted to create a system which could handle the potential business quickly, so that they could be the first into the new market. They bought IEF and JMA spent six months building the system for them, and one month testing it. When the law was finally changed on a Friday, Nykredit was able to go live with the system on the following Monday.

The financial services industry is a huge source of potential business for a company like JMA, since the industry lives or dies by the technology which it installs and the way in which it uses it. In Britain, Barclays Bank was one of the first customers for IEF.

The bank wanted to find a way of building its new Global Banking System which would control the cost of developing computer systems. The Global Banking System, a single, seamless, world-wide service for corporate customers, consists of software which will allow data to be managed, transactions processed and reports prepared and transmitted. When it is installed, in 1990, Barclays will be able to run its entire global network on a branch network basis. IEF seemed less document-heavy to them, and more understandable to the users than anything else on the market. They needed it in order to control the development of their computer systems, since the price of failure in financial information technology projects is horribly high. Poor coding and poor testing are bad enough; mistakes in the early stages of a project, when the problem is being analysed and systems are being designed, can cause months or even years of costly delays. Once up and running 80 per cent of subsequent maintenance work in traditional systems has to be carried out as a result of faults in the initial analysis and specification.

The Banque Cantonale Vaudoise (BCV) in Switzerland was another early customer for the product. The headquarters of BCV are terraced into the hillside above Lac Leman in Lausanne, a suitably glamorous setting. It is the eighth largest in the Swiss banking league, which makes it a successful but medium-sized local player in a market which is dominated by international giants. It has assets of £3.5 billion and 380,000 customers, but the senior managers were worried about how well the bank would fare if world trading conditions became any tougher, particularly with increased competition coming from areas like America and Japan.

Due to restrictions in law, cantonal banks are not allowed to set up branches outside their own area, although they can accept international business via arrangements with overseas partners.

To meet the challenges of tough future trading and the approaching 'one market' of 1992, the BCV managers wanted to improve the bank's performance by establishing links with other cantonal banks within Switzerland, and by finding ways to compete abroad. The bank's ageing computer systems, however, were not fit to cope with such a challenge. Their data processing department was unable to supply information quickly and easily about customer profitability and there was little systems support even for the bank's limited stock-market activities. They could not, in other words, give their managers the information needed for decision-making.

The IEF enabled BCV to construct a computer model of a busines strategy so that its strengths and weaknesses can be analysed and the activities which have to be in place for its successful implementation identified. It will also generate automatically the programs necessary to support the business once the strategy has been agreed.

In six months JMA constructed a comprehensive five-year information systems strategy, based on the new business objectives laid down by the bank's board of directors. It integrated its business strategy and its information systems strategy so tightly that the bank could feel confident that the computer systems necessary would be in place when needed. It meant redeveloping their strategies from scratch, but also meant that they could keep track of detail and eliminate errors.

The system holds in its memory a comprehensive set of rules for the way the business operates and will not let the planners break those rules or put in place new initiatives without proper systems back-up.

The bank was won over to the system by their senior vice president who attended a James Martin seminar and was converted to the cause. He proved a powerful inside salesman for the consultancy and for IEF.

The IEF product is owned by TI, so although JMA had established their consultancy in the US, TI retained the marketing rights for the product there, but gave them to JMA for Europe.

Although the American arm of JMA does not have the revenue earning potential of the IEF, it has the advantage of working within the biggest consulting market in the world. As well as being able to support other manufacturers, JMA is also able to support TI with installations, and help to sell the concept of information engineering to senior managers.

Although the operation is slightly different from the European companies, JMA in America is working in the world's largest CASE technology market. The size of this opportunity for JMA was inestimable but, as with all major steps forward, there were some enormous hurdles to be jumped and precipices to be avoided. When a minnow like JMA gets into bed with a giant like TI, it is all too easy to get squashed in your sleep. They were going to have to remain more alert than they realized in the coming months.

'FAIRBRAIN'

JOINING THE ESTABLISHMENT

- Restructuring the company to sell products as well as services.

- Becoming a medium-sized company.

- Changing management gear and changing the leader.

- As a company grows it must adapt its philosophies to suit the changing situation— If it is growing fast it must change fast.

In 1963, while Jim Martin was formulating his theories and gaining his early experience at IBM, an eager young marketing executive was setting sail for New York from Britain. David Fairbairn had been charged by his employers, the Guinness company, with the setting up of a marketing operation in America for their famous beer.

Many years later Martin was to appoint David to take over from Tony Carter as the worldwide head of JMA. A more different man from Tony it would be hard to imagine. David is a deeply intellectual, calculating man, with none of Tony's rough edges, but he had learnt about industry from the bottom up. Behind the bespectacled smile David has a will of steel, with all his decisions based on computations. His colleagues nicknamed him 'Fairbrain'.

Back in the 1960s Guinness had had experiences within the American market which had been less than successful, and had left them wary. David had been working in their overseas advertising and marketing department and had suggested to the powers that were, that they should try again to actually set up their own US operation in order to exploit the huge potential market effectively. He himself had already had international experience of setting up new operations for them in Malaysia and Nigeria. Showing considerable faith in the abilities of such a young man, or possibly in the hope of shutting him up, Guinness told him to go and do it, starting from scratch.

He arrived in New York with virtually nothing and within a couple of months he had bought a house and two cars, rented an office on Third Avenue and hired himself a secretary and a bookkeeper. By the time he left America six years later his operation was turning over £20m, and was the second largest beer distributor in the country. More importantly, David Fairbairn had become fascinated by the power of computers as management tools, and adept at using them.

In the early 1960s computers were still talked about in much the same way as robots and space travel. Everyone knew it was happening, but didn't actually want anything to do with it themselves. Technofear was a major stumbling block, particularly among senior managers who had not received any training on machines, and who didn't feel able to handle such a major change in the way they did things.

Only a visionary few could see what a big business the computing industry was going to turn into, and what massive power would be opened up to anyone who could understand how to use computers to plan and run a business. At that stage Guinness, a staid and traditional British company, had only just installed their first mainframe at their Park Royal headquarters in England, and it took some hard talking for David to convince them that he needed a computer to set up his virtually non-existent operation in the New World.

Finally they agreed to the idea and he purchased an early IBM 360 system. IBM offered to give him an Executive Familiarization Course, a very necessary adjunct to the selling of computers in those days, even more so than now, but he decided that the standard course would only scrape the surface of the knowledge which he wanted to acquire, and that he wanted to go more deeply into the subject. The manufacturers weren't geared up to help him any further and he realized that he was going to have to find a way of educating himself.

He looked around for a course that would teach him as much as it was possible to know at the time, and ended up enrolling at an adult education college in Long Island. Every evening for four months, when he finished work in his Manhattan office, he headed out to night school on the Island to find out how to programme a computer so that it would help plan and run his business for him. It was hard work, but it wasn't a chore, since the subject was beginning to take a grip on his imagination. Initially he planned to learn enough to understand for himself exactly what the computer could do, before he hired a computer manager to handle the day-to-day running of the system. That way he felt he would be able to direct the manager more clearly and confidently, and would be able to understand the information that was going in and coming out of the system.

During the learning process, however, he became seduced and enthralled by the capabilities of the machines, and obviously had a natural aptitude for the subject. Half-way through the course he decided that he would not hire a computer manager at all, but would do the job himself. At that time the idea of a company president actually programming his own computer was so unheard of that a business magazine ran a profile of him, explaining what he was doing to an amazed readership.

The fascination for him came from being able to develop a system, knowing exactly what he wanted it to do. Whereas most professional programmers are working in a vacuum, hoping that they are creating products which people will find useful, he was a working manager who knew precisely what would be useful and valuable, and then setting out to find ways to achieve it.

With his IBM machine he was able to perform what seemed like magical management feats, which today might seem commonplace within sophisticated multinational companies, but then were unheard of. He was able to organize his whole selling structure around what the computer was capable of. He could see exactly how much stock had sold at any one time, and could break down income in innumerable different combinations. He could measure the effects of an advertisement almost instantly and adjust his advertising campaign on the strength of the results, avoiding wasting money on bad ideas and making capital out of good ones.

When the American operation was up and running for Guinness, he returned to Britain, but soon began to question whether he was working in the right environment. He had caught the 'high-tech' bug and Guinness was not a company which was ever likely to keep itself at the leading edge of technology. He had to get closer to the action so he moved on to ICL, where he was an unusual asset, being an expert who had acquired his experience as a user, and who had actually had an opportunity to take his ideas up from scratch.

At ICL he worked on mainframe marketing, before moving on to Thorn EMI to work on the launch of their body-brain scanner in 1976. From a standing start the scanner was earning £100 million a year within four years, and David had had another taste of the excitement of building a company from nothing, and the satisfaction of seeing it take off in a big way.

By 1980 he was becoming a well-known figure in the computing establishment, and he was invited to be Director of the National Computing Centre. In 1982 he was involved in the Alvey Programme, which was the government-funded research programme launched in response to the Japanese challenge from fifth-generation computers. The work was done in collaboration with universities and industry, and one of the activities which they researched was software engineering.

David was also fascinated by the emergence of the micro-computer as a powerful contender for the business market. He bought himself a Tandy, and went back to hammering away into the night in order to learn how to program it to machine code level. Again he became entranced with the possibilities of what he could make it do. He set up a Micro Centre at the NCC and was involved in introducing micros into schools. He brought together some of the most interesting people in the field as technical advisers. One of them, John Fairclough was then a vice president at IBM and has since gone on to be scientific adviser to the British Cabinet Office. At the time John expressed his astonishment that his company was being so slow at moving into the micro business. Soon afterwards, of course, IBM realized its mistake and went from a standing start to dominating the sector in about fourteen months. What fascinated men like this was the degree of responsiveness which was possible with the new generation of machines. The businessman could make them do almost anything to meet his needs.

David believed that the problem in the software engineering field was that it was 'all supply and no marketing'. The industry needed to promote itself and its messages better to the outside business world. He put together a user panel to look at the problems. Software engineering was then still at a very early stage, and although the Japanese had recognized its importance, the West still hadn't woken up to it. David then opened a software engineering department at the NCC, feeling certain that it was the most important single component of high-technology research activity, even more important than chip-technology research.

He studied over 100 programs in the field, selecting a shortlist of 36, of which only 6 actually seemed to match up to what he knew the market was looking for. There were some major industrial users on his research panel, and all of them seemed uncomfortable with the programs which were being produced.

One of the members of the panel was from Rolls Royce, and he mentioned to David that he had come across a company offering a maverick view which they were calling information engineering. The company was JMA. Although David was very familiar with Jim Martin, whose advice had been sought at various stages in the Alvey Programme, he had not come across JMA. His contact at Rolls Royce told him that the managers at JMA took a different view of the whole idea, starting with the central component—the concept—rather than with the tools. They began at the strategic level, devising tools and implementing techniques to achieve strategic goals. It was an approach that worked from the top down, and David immediately felt that he had stumbled across something important.

He wrote to the company for their literature and made contact with Tony Carter. At that time Tony was looking for a managing director for his UK operation. The two of them got on well, and David's contract with the NCC was coming up for renewal. The NCC had asked him to stay, but he thought the time had come to move on. He suggested himself for the job at JMA and Tony was delighted. For about six months David divided his time equally between the NCC and JMA, and came on board full time in 1985.

Unlike the other entrepreneurs in the group, David was taking over an existing company. At that stage it was being run by Malcolm Coster, who then went over to running the products division. Malcolm had been recruited by Tony from BP to take over the UK operation from him. Tony courted Malcolm assiduously for five years, using all his best trapline methods. Malcolm's strength was his understanding of the politics of large corporate entities, the sort of people who were JMA's clients. He had a significant effect on the character of the fast-growing young consultancy. Unfortunately Malcolm was also used to a more professional style of management. He was a strong character and did not hesitate to speak out when he disagreed with things that Tony was doing. Within six months he and Tony had fallen out.

According to Tony the problem was that Malcolm had never before had to worry about things like cashflow, and that he brought big company politics with him. For whatever reasons Malcolm was not enjoying JMA, and his disillusionment with Tony looked as if it was going to spread through the company. Tony began to rally support from his fellow managers to fire Malcolm. Despite being well respected within the company as a manager, Malcolm finally left to return to a big company atmosphere. He joined Coopers and Lybrand and quickly demonstrated just how able a manager he was when working with the right team.

JMA had reached its most interesting stage of development. There was a row of books on information engineering methodologies ready to go into use, and steps were being taken with TI to move to the second stage by automating the product. The company faced the tough proposition of changing from pure consultancy to selling products. It was exactly the sort of situation which David found exciting. It reminded him of the start-up of the Guinness operation and of the Thorn EMI Scanner. He felt he was in at the beginning of something very big indeed. He knew all about product marketing, and he was also able to bring his experience of the computing establishment to bear. He was a fellow of the British Computer Society, as well as having all his contacts at the NCC. He was on the board of the British Standards Institute and was chairman of the Information Technology Council. He was vice chairman of the Government Committee on Standards and on the Monopolies Commission. He was exactly the sort of 'establishment' figure who could complement Tony Carter's image of salesmanship and entrepreneurism.

The company was now reaching a level where not everyone on the staff could be billed out every day. When a consultancy reaches a certain size it is inevitable that it has to start hiring administrative and managerial staff who do not actively generate income, but without whom the consultants who do bring in the money couldn't function.

David did very little billable work himself. His time was taken up just managing the launch of the product marketing operation. Initially he split the UK company very definitely between product sales and consulting, but once the operation was fired up and working well, he merged them back together again, giving the sales people, or 'business development' people, responsibility for the total delivery of a solution. Although they are still doing a hard sell, they are now selling a complete package, including all the consultancy work.

Whereas at the launch of IEF the company reckoned that they would be able to sell an average of £120,000-worth of consultancy work on the back of a £200,000 IEF sale, they have since found that in practice the IEF sale brings in far more than its own worth in consultancy and training fees.

As the UK business grew it became divided up between the north and south of Britain, with the opening of an office in Nottingham based on the business being handled for Shell and Barclays in the area. The Nottingham office had grown to thirteen people by 1989. The Scandinavian market also became active, which led to a conflict of interests between Cor Swart, who believed that all of Europe should be his territory, and David who wanted to handle the business from the UK where it had originated. The 'Kings' which Tony had created were beginning to war over territories, and it began to look as if those, like Ian Palmer, who thought it was time to restructure the company along more sophisticated, multinational lines, might be right. Tony sided with David and rather than opening offices in each of the Scandinavian capitals the business continued to be managed from the UK.

One of the difficulties facing David was in fusing together the efforts of the very different characters who made up the selling and consultancy teams.

Good salespeople tend to be very focused and persevering. They can get an objective in view and be terrier-like in pursuing it. They are generally very interested in money and are selfish to a degree, in that they are mainly interested in their own objectives. They need to be highly organized people, and although they do not necessarily need to be deeply conversant with the technology, they need to be good interpreters. They are totally customer-orientated.

The consultants, on the other hand, all have to have a genuine, in-depth knowledge of the product. Their main motivation, beyond bringing in a profit, must be to achieve the highest possible quality of work. The trick for a good manager is to balance these two diverse elements.

In the beginning the consultants were expected to go out and find their own customers. As the company grew and became more sophisticated, and the marketing function evolved with the job of identifying potential customers and knocking on their doors, the salespeople were then needed to go in to qualify the prospects. Because the best prospects come from existing consultancy jobs, salespeople are allocated groups of clients to work on.

In 1988 the staff in the UK company doubled from 64 to 124, where they had predicted a rise to 89, and they had produced a £1m profit. The managers who had shares in the company were beginning to realize that on paper they were becoming rich men.

As companies grow they are forced to go through certain gear changes. It was becoming clear to many of the senior management that JMA, worldwide, needed a different style of management from the one which it had been using for its foundation. It needed an elaborately calculated strategy if it was to achieve the potential which Martin had been predicting for the 1990s.

Every so often the company's management holds 'JAM sessions' (the name originated from a misprint of the initials JMA, and stuck), where every member of the company is taken away for the weekend, and the managers take the opportunity to do some serious communicating on where the company is going and why. One of these events was held in Eastbourne, and Tony made his theme 'profit, profit, profit'; a chant which he set up from the stage and which he suggested other managers should include in their speeches. The reasoning was that the company needed to be as profitable as possible in order to float it on the stock market.

The many who were made shareholders by Tony could see the point of his argument. Others in the audience, however, thought it was too soon to adopt this strategy with so many exciting opportunities on the horizon which might increase the value of the company radically in the long-term. Some thought that if Tony was keen to float and capitalize his shares before the majority were ready, perhaps he might manage the company with an undesirably short-term view. There were rumblings of concern, and whenever anyone posed the question; 'If Tony left who would replace him?', the name David Fairbairn always seemed to come up. He, it was thought, would be able to give the company the far-sighted strategic direction which it needed; he had the weight and gravity necessary to run a major multinational consultancy. At that stage, however, it was still only idle speculation.

Although a flotation was beginning to look like an unrealistic prospect in the short-term, Tony did indeed want to sell the company. Having reached his fiftieth birthday he was beginning to want to wind down and to enjoy some of the fruits of his success. He began to talk to several potential buyers who had been attracted by JMA's sudden, dramatic growth in profits. He was being encouraged by the venture capitalists who were eager to cash in with a massive return on investment. Neither Martin nor the rest of the senior team wanted to sell the company, believing that it was on the brink of an enormous expansion phase.

Tony Carter was a brilliant entrepreneur. His expertise was in getting things started. Without him JMA would not have come into existence. Once the company was up and running he became busy creating a sports management company. He needed the start-up situation and challenge to excite him. JMA had changed and it needed a different type of executive to deal with it, someone who would not become bored by the daily detail of running a big company.

Martin knew how critical it had been to replace Don Brown years earlier and wondered if the time had come for a change at the very top of JMA.

In June 1989 Tony went on holiday in Portugal while the management team met behind closed doors to discuss the 1990s. He had made a surprising decision not to attend the meeting, acknowledging that he disagreed with the general strategy now favoured by the other managers. They didn't believe that now was the right time to be maximizing profits at the expense of growth. It was a time for investing in the future and concentrating on growth. They knew that the future was going to be dramatic in its complexity and opportunities. They felt there were new things that they could do, new products and services which they could create which would continue the company's dramatic growth rate. While Tony recognised the need for research and development he felt he could plan and budget for it within his strategy of profitability, which included funding through third-party involvement.

During the meeting the management team decided that their position was so far from Tony's that it would be difficult to support him any longer as CEO. When Tony called the financial director Tom Underhill to be debriefed after the meeting he listened quietly to their decisions and announced his intention of resigning as CEO. He asked them to propose a plan which would buy the majority of his shares and reposition him as a board director outside the executive management committee.

Tony's decision was a difficult one for him to live with, although everybody knew it was the right one to take. With so much of his style based upon personal relationships it hurt him deeply to take himself off the team. He reacted in a characteristic way and withdrew inside his hard outer shell, allowing only his wife Susan to understand his true feelings.

David Fairbairn became the world chief executive officer, while Tony sold most of his shares in a deal worth close to £3 million. The press was as surprised as the rest of the industry. One paper carried the headline—RUGGER DEBUGGER QUITS.

THE FINANCIAL MINEFIELD

LOOKING OVER THE PRECIPICE

- Restructuring the finances.

- Dealing with the venture capitalists.

- When the stakes become higher you stand the chance of winning the jackpot—or of losing more than you would initially have thought possible.

- To grow, a company must take risks. To learn, a company must make mistakes. If either the risks or the mistakes are too great the company is out of business. If not they have made it to the big time.

- When a professional financier lends you money he is concerned first with his money and only secondly with you.

In the summer of 1984 an American conglomerate called Esmark was taken over by Beatrice Foods. Esmark was one of those corporations that few people have heard of, even though it was a $12 billion company owning names like Avis, Max Factor and Playtex. At that time they also had a young international director of operational analysis called Tom Underhill.

After the takeover it looked as if Tom was going to have to move to the company's new European headquarters in Brussels. It wasn't a move he relished, so he decided to look around at the job market. An advertisement in the *Financial Times* alerted him to the fact that a young company called JMA was looking for a group financial controller. He went down to Wimbledon to meet Tony Carter and find out about the job.

Tony put across his usual bullish message, 'selling' the company to the potential new recruit. The JMA message sounded exciting to Tom. It looked like a company which was going to grow fast, and he was being offered an opportunity to grow with it. Although he was only 29 his experience of working within a giant company, with all the financial checks and systems which are involved, was attractive to Tony. If JMA was going to grow as fast as he wanted it to, it was going to need directors who knew how to set up and run a big organization, and who also had enough fire in their bellies to push the company through the painful early growing stages.

Had Tom realized just what a bumpy ride he was in for he might not have been quite so keen to follow Tony over the top. Suddenly he found himself working with an entrepreneur who, when faced with a strategic decision, did not 'model it', as he would have done at Esmark, to test which would be the best route to follow, he simply followed his gut feelings. On the whole his hunches turned out to be right, but to someone who had been commercially trained within the rigorous confines of a major organization it seemed undisciplined and dangerous.

Tom, however, had wanted to be in charge and responsible for the finances of a company, and that meant starting with a small operation and growing with it, hoping that enough of the gut feelings which the management team had were right. Virtually any start-up operation is under-funded and flying by the seat of its pants for at least a few years. Within weeks of arriving Tom realized that he had a stake in a company which could very well still succumb to cot death. They were continuing to grow at 80 per cent a year, which meant they were having to invest heavily to support the growth, which meant that their balance sheet was particularly weak.

Whereas in his previous job he was used to at least one bank a week inviting him out to lunch in the hope of winning Esmark business, banks didn't even want to handle JMA's business at some stages. Only once they had passed the magic £1 million profit figure did he find he started to receive positive bankers' telephone calls again.

Although he felt serious doubts about how the company would survive, those doubts never became greater than his faith in what the company had set out to do. After eighteen months the danger of cot death had passed, and the company seemed more to him like a spotty adolescent, bursting with potential but no profits, and during 1988 it grew up into a balanced, healthy adult.

Handling the finances of a small, fast-growing company is not everyone's cup of tea. In order to demonstrate that you are an exceptional finance director you need to show that you have complete control over the whole group. With a loosely based group of entrepreneurs, building a company at 80 per cent a year, that is close to impossible. The trick is to develop a close working relationship with the CEO and to operate as a team. Tom and Tony formed just such a relationship.

A number of problems confronted Tom when he first joined JMA. Firstly the company had to be brought on-shore from Bermuda, where Tony and Jim had first set it up. Being an off-shore company was not good for their image in the City, and they now needed to woo the money-men if they were to get the venture capital they needed and even float the company in the future. Being registered in Bermuda was also likely to aggravate the British tax authorities unnecessarily once the company started making sizeable profits. Until then they had only been exporting losses, which did not worry anyone except Tom.

At the same time Tom had to negotiate for the buy-out of Dixon Doll— a particularly acrimonious and litigious process; deal with the venture capitalists who were being approached to provide the necessary funds to take JMA up to the next stage of its development, and handle other aspects of the company's growth, like the finding and funding of new premises. He also had to mediate between Tony, who had no respect at all for people like venture capitalists, and the bankers and investors whose help they needed. It was a time of transition when the young entrepreneurial start-up operation was maturing into a sizeable company.

From the beginning Martin had had an agreement with Tony which had been made to protect both of them. The ratio of their shares in the company was fixed and unchangeable. This eliminated any financial scheming between them. Neither could get the better of the other financially. Unfortunately it also prevented Martin from increasing his investment in the company unless Carter did likewise, and Carter did not have the money to do that. That meant that the funds were going to have to come from outside. The contract had seemed prudent to Martin at the beginning, although in retrospect he admits it was a mistake. He believes that there should not have been any necessity to go to the venture capitalists. Martin should have financed JMA's growth himself, but the contract prevented this happening.

Initially the JMA management were unsure how much money they needed for funding their development. Tony believed they should be able to do it out of cashflow, Malcolm and Ian felt that it would be necessary to look at other sources. Tony had already talked to a few contacts of his own, but nothing substantial had emerged.

Discussions with Warburgs suggested that JMA needed a deal which would allow them to draw down £1.7 million, working on the theory that most borrowers end up needing twice as much as they start out asking for. Warburgs didn't want to fund the whole deal themselves and brought in Charterhouse Japhet who, in turn, led to Syntech, and a three-way loan was arranged. Despite all their doubts about taking money from venture capitalists, the JMA management team found there were benefits to having such established names behind them. It gave the company credibility in the eyes of clients to have established financial institutions showing themselves willing to back them. It allayed any fears they might have that the company would disappear midway through a major contract.

The next difficulty was caused, as so often happens in small companies, by their own success. The deal with TI to market IEF was such a huge opportunity that it couldn't be ignored, but it completely changed the potential nature of the company, particularly in the UK. Whereas a giant like TI could very easily finance the development and marketing of a product of this size from their cashflow, it marked a major departure for a consultancy which had been surviving, for only a few years, almost solely on the daily fees earned by its consultants.

When JMA knew that it was going to be given the rights to market IEF as soon as it was ready, decisions had to be made about how to restructure the company to take on this major new commitment. Initially it was decided to split it into two, maintaining the consultancy operation and creating a brand new product division. Information Engineering Products (IEP) was created as a separate company. It would later be merged back into JMA.

In order to build an experienced sales operation, and to become established in the marketplace, the management decided to take on the distribution rights for a number of products in the software engineering field. They wanted to build the team's expertise in readiness for the arrival of IEF, and improve their own cashflow in the interim.

To start with the strategy worked well. They won the agency for Excelerator, an analysis workbench which, although a CASE tool, was not comprehensive, and a code generator called APS. The products were good, although not in the same league as the approaching IEF; the sales team worked hard and the money started rolling in. JMA began to win industry awards, like the ICP Award 'A million in one' for Excelerator, which means achieving a million dollars worth of sales on a product in the first year. It became the market leader in several European countries.

The Excelerator was made by a company called Intech, which Jim had invested in. The connection came when Ian Palmer and Malcolm Coster were visiting Jim in Vermont and he was talking about projects he was involved in. Ian's attention was caught by the idea of Excelerator and he suggested that JMA should sell it in Europe. Jim rang Intech's chairman Rich Carpenter and put him on the 'phone to the other two. The idea was agreed in principle there and then.

David Fairbairn's previous experience in marketing and management was proving invaluable. Unfortunately the company was being too successful and the manufacturers of the agency products began to ask questions about JMA's longer term strategies. IEF was beginning to emerge and be talked about, particularly because of Jim Martin's established views on the need for integrated CASE tools. Since Excelerator was not integrated, the manufacturers believed there would be an inevitable clash of interests. They issued an ultimatum, IEF or them, and the other manufacturers soon followed their lead. The management at JMA had to make a major decision.

They were just into a new financial year, and all their predictions had been made on the assumption that they would continue to build a thriving agency business for at least another year. IEF was not yet ready for launching, but there was no doubt that when it did come out it would be massively important, and was an integral part of Jim's philosophy, which was the cornerstone of JMA. If the agency products went, so would 40 per cent of JMA's predicted revenue for the year.

On top of this the company's finances were being badly affected by the mistakes which were then being made in America. Some recruiting mistakes had proved expensive and the products business had become more costly in its early stages than had been anticipated.

Application Builder was a complex code generator which a programmer called Terry Wilcox had been working on for some years. It was still not finished but Terry managed to convince Tony that it would not take much effort to make it marketable. Tony decided to go out and sell the product, using the revenue which it generated to do the necessary work. It soon became evident that it would cost hundreds of thousands, if not millions, to get the product right. JMA was haemorrhaging money, and Application Builder had to be axed.

The financial situation at JMA was growing critical and Tony became uncharacteristically withdrawn. For three weeks he held out, even though his own house was on the line if the company went down. Finally he had to confront the problem.

A difficult decision was made and, being a small company, they were able to respond quickly to the problem. The agency products were going to have to be allowed to go and, if possible, the launch of IEF in Europe would have to be brought forward, which would mean taking a few technical risks with the product.

JMA decided to follow TI's lead and launch the IEF under a beta-test programme. This meant they were able to deliver the analyses and design workbenches with the control encyclopaedia first, and with the code generator following later.

TI were still working on the IEF product, and refused to be rushed. They were determined to get it right before launching the complete product. By this time there was a development team of 60 people working full time on the project. When the marketing contract was signed with JMA in February 1985, TI were still not sure whether there was actually going to be a product. They were finally persuaded to make the first beta-test in 1986 in the States and then in Europe (a beta-test is when a client agrees to buy a product at a lesser price, in the knowledge that it is not yet fully completed and is still in its early stages), but IEF did not become fully commercially available until 1987.

Even before the problems with the agency products arose, relations with the venture capitalists were turning sour. It takes a lot more capital for a company to break into the product business than the consultancy business. It was no longer going to be possible for JMA to keep up the juggling act with the contracts staying just ahead of the payroll. To launch IEF comfortably they would have to find more capital, and the only source looked as if it would be the venture capital companies. Tony was not keen. He did not like the strings that were attached to all venture capital in Britain. He was used to getting his own way and he still believes that at the time the backers agreed to give them the money, JMA could have survived without it, but from that moment on it became a self-fulfilling prophecy that they couldn't manage without it.

His entrepreneurial experience told him that venture capitalists made little effort to understand the businesses which they invest in. He wanted to fund the money out of cashflow, from the income which had been generated by the products they were selling under agency.

His philosophy had always been that if you bill more each month than you spend, you can always raise extra money from the bank if you need it. The euphoric expectations generated by the approach of the IEF launch, however, and his own unfamiliarity with the product market, lulled him into disobeying his instincts. At that stage they had pulled back from the brink and everyone on the team felt bullish and impatient to get going. They decided to borrow enough money to launch IEF in style, and to make contacts which would give them future access to the funds of the City should they require more.

Tony firmly believed that if they were given the go-ahead for the money by a lender, they would instantly spend it, even before they had been given it. It is syndrome well-known in Britain, the Government having done the same with the revenues from North Sea Oil, so that all the money was spent long before the oil actually came out of the seabed. In the event this also proved to be true at JMA. By the time the money was actually delivered they really needed it, because it was already committed. For a short while, Tony believed, they became a little 'fat and happy', lulled into that state by their new backers.

His partners, however, persuaded him that they needed the money for marketing and recruitment, so Tony agreed. None of the three companies which came up with the money was able to persuade Tony that venture capitalists were good for a business. As the relationships developed his partners began to see his point of view more clearly. Before long the major part of every board meeting was taken up with the question of how to buy out the backers.

> When venture capitalists back an entrepreneur, [Tony said later],
> the first thing they want to do is remove his power because he is
> too strong for them. The relationship starts with a honeymoon
> period, when everyone is pleased with the match. Then something
> goes wrong and they try to divide and conquer, undermining the
> entrepreneur and trying to isolate him from his other directors.
> In the end the British venture capitalists seem to be too greedy.

The backers, not surprisingly, like to make their money as safe as possible, that means that they like to see the companies they invest in put in as many controls as possible. That is the way that many of the really big companies work successfully, but it tends to stifle creativity and lead to lost opportunities. It is opportunities which are the life blood of growing companies like JMA; they have to be free to grab them quickly. The two sides did not mix well.

A backer may decide that a company is worth investing in because of its management philosophy. If, as at JMA, the philosophy is a 'people' one, it may include motivating factors like paying generous bonuses. Once the backers are onboard they see those bonuses as cutting directly into their profits, and they begin to want to see some changes made.

The team at JMA had also believed that their backers would help them in other ways such as finding new business, perhaps with introductions to the managing directors or financial directors of other companies who could become clients. No such help was forthcoming despite promises to the contrary, either because the backers didn't have the contacts (which seemed unlikely given their reputations), or because they didn't have sufficient faith in JMA to recommend them.

Tony saw a wide difference in attitude between the UK and the US. In America the backers seem to expect that ten investments will produce three successful companies, three mediocre ones and four that will go under. In Britain they do not want to lose any, so they spend more time on trying to save the four they are going to lose anyway than on helping the top three, which are the ones that could actually make them a lot of money.

Martin, who has worked extensively with US venture capitalists, had also observed the best of the breed truly helping the companies that they invested in—helping them to acquire the right management teams, to fill in any organizational holes, to build the necessary finance and marketing skills, to get the numbers right in order to maximize the value when they went public. Like many other entrepreneurs operating in the UK, he believes that Britain badly needs to develop a venture capital infrastructure like the best parts of the US system. JMA's investors gave the company no practical help.

Tony did in fact talk to American venture capitalists as well, many of whom were interested in the company, but they did not want to invest in Britain, so the company was forced to go to British lenders.

The three companies JMA was dealing with agreed to lend a total of £1.7 million. JMA actually borrowed £850,000 in two stages and were going to draw down a third payment of £400,000. But by the time it came to the third stage JMA had hit its problems with the agency products being withdrawn; now the backers were going to be put to the test. Would they run for cover, or would they stand behind the company which they had professed to have faith in when everything was going smoothly?

There was no doubt that it was a difficult time for the company, and it was not surprising that the backers became nervous. Instead of rallying round to help JMA, which was what the company had expected them to do, the backers said that they were going to have to change the terms of the loans. They were basically raising the price of the final part of the loan because they didn't think things looked as smooth as they had at the beginning. For JMA the money they were being offered did not look at all attractive, particularly since they were already feeling the pinch in loss of cashflow. To take on even more debt at such a time did not seem sensible. The last part of the loan had become far too expensive in terms of equity to be feasible, but it looked as if they were going to be forced by circumstances to accept it. It is a problem faced by anyone who is down on their luck. Should they borrow money from a loan shark at exorbitant rates, knowing that they will have trouble paying back the interest in the future?

Just at the moment when they felt they needed help and support, JMA were being squeezed for even more. After some agonizing soul-searching they took their courage in both hands and turned the money down. Had they taken up that final £400,000, the backers would, in effect, have multiplied their original money tenfold in just two years. As it was their initial £850,000, which was convertible into shares, was already worth an estimated £3 million by the end of 1988. The relationships had become badly soured on both sides.

With no other outside source of financial help and Tony refusing to change his contract with Jim, it was a time for strong nerves at JMA. As happened before, they had spent this final payment in anticipation of receiving it, and were consequently in some trouble when they decided to do without it. They were short of £700,000 on the day that they declined to take up the loan. The cash had to be found from somewhere. Tony called together his managers and explained the situation. Each one of them went away and looked at every avenue for cost cutting. It was like taking the company back to its roots, fighting to stay in business and to keep afloat until the money started to come in again. They negotiated with suppliers for credit, rearranged royalty payments, chased customers for payment, arranged advance payments and moved all the figures that it was legally possible to move around the group. Within six weeks the £700,000 had been found, and the extra equity holding which the backers would have been able to walk away with had been saved, to go back into the company and into the paychecks of the employees.

One of the conditions which the backers insisted on at the beginning of the relationship was installing a non-executive vice chairman on the board, to act as their ears and eyes. They sent three or four potential candidates to meet Tony, none of whom was capable of working for a company like JMA. Most of them seemed to Tony to be in the 'retired admiral' class of director, hardly suitable for a company wanting to stay on the leading edge of the fastest moving industry on earth.

One weekend Tony was at home watching *The Money Programme* on television. Robert Maxwell had just won a takeover battle with Extel and had ousted director Alan Brooker. In an interview on the programme Alan said that he was looking for companies in which to take a non-executive interest. Tony liked the sound of him and they met for a drink. After a few such meetings they discovered they had a great deal in common, and Alan, who proved himself to be acceptable to the backers, joined as vice chairman. JMA had a valuable new board member able to advise and bring new ideas to the company, as well as helping Tony in meetings with senior executives and from a management point of view acting as the chairman of the company.

The whole group believes in the value of having non-executive directors on the boards in all the various countries. They provide a number of benefits. In some cases it is a question of contacts, with the non-executive directors coming from high-level jobs in industry, government or the armed forces. In other cases they help with recruitment, being university professors and lecturers, and some of them will also be equipped to take on some consulting work, or to advise the boards on the laws of their countries. Their presence on the various boards is a discipline, encouraging JMA managers and directors to think and work like the clients they are servicing.

Eventually, after Tony had left the company, Martin became free to increase his ownership. He acquired a controlling interest, buying out most of the venture capitalists' shares. He was putting his own money behind his strong beliefs that JMA is set to grow vigorously over the next decade.

THE BIG LAUNCH

FROM SELLING TO MARKETING

- Moving from trapline selling to sophisticated 'big ticket' marketing.

- If a company can't sell its products or services it doesn't exist. If it is successful at selling it will grow into the sort of company which needs marketing plans rather than sales pitches.

- How to launch a new product with a minimum price tag of £250,000.

The launch of IEF was heralded with a blaze of publicity. Public relations consultants, Wickes and Associates were hired, and articles appeared on the front and back pages of the *Financial Times*, in the *Sunday Times* and other prime media. It was an extraordinarily successful press campaign, worth hundreds of thousands of pounds in free advertising. Everyone in the information technology industry could see the colossal value of such a tool. By being the first ones out with an integrated CASE tool JMA were able to establish the market, taking the high ground away from the competition and giving themselves an authoritative voice. To the business people who understood such things, it seemed that the much heralded 'information age' had finally arrived.

Almost immediately it became apparent that not only were JMA going to be able to shrug off their financial problems of the previous year, they were suddenly sitting on top of a very successful company indeed.

All the prime movers in the company, who had been enticed in by Tony with equity had, on paper at least, become wealthy men.

It had, however, been a hard transition period for the company, not only financially. While JMA had been working purely as consultants, all the marketing could be done at a local level. With products it became more complex. International pricing strategies had to be worked out, and marketing guidelines had to become consistent throughout the group. In consultancy the best marketing policy is to let the consultant who is going to be handling the project do the selling. In the product area this is not possible.

A top-flight marketing manager needed to be found for the holding company and Stephen Izatt, who had experience working out in California's Silicon Valley, was recruited to co-ordinate the international marketing efforts—a difficult job in a company which had grown up with a philosophy of Country Manager is King.

Product marketing skills had to be introduced into the UK company to handle the launch and follow-up of the IEF product. Priced at around a quarter of a million pounds it was an expensive product. Even in the world of computer software, where companies are used to writing large cheques, this was a lot of money to ask customers to pay for a new, and largely untested, idea. It required some heavy-duty marketing expertise. Tony, being a true-blue salesman, had always been sceptical about the value of marketing until then. He recognized the need to hire some good people.

There were a limited number of potential customers at that stage who were in a position to buy IEF. So the marketing team started by writing to each of them. The UK marketing team hired the penthouse on the top of the Tower Hotel, with its spectacular views over the City, Docklands and the River Thames, and invited the information technology directors of around 50 of the top 200 companies to attend seminars there, at which IEF could be explained to them.

At that high level of management, it was relatively easy to explain exactly what the benefits of the system were. JMA could highlight the problems which they knew all the companies had, and could then show them how IEF would solve them. The nuts-and-bolts questions of how to get it to work could be left to people lower down the managerial ladder.

By November 1987 IEF had been sold to Rank Xerox, John Lewis, the Post Office, Avis, Barclays Bank and Rolls Royce. It was a stunning success record, considering the usual gestation period for sales of this size. With each sale there followed a requirement for consultancy work to help the client to install. The Tower Hotel seminar was also taken to other business centres like Edinburgh and into Scandinavia, with equal degrees of success.

Recruitment became critical if all the installations were to receive a good service, since the company had to find consultants who were good enough to live up to the promise of the product. Massive recruitment days were held at the Dorchester, the hotel where the whole story had started just seven years before. Fifty people would be interviewed in a day to find the necessary eighteen or nineteen recruits.

Good consultants were keen to work for the company now. JMA's image in the marketplace was established. The publicity caused by the IEF launch had lifted the company's profile and it was now seen as one of the key players in a new, exciting area.

While the group has now grown into a sophisticated organization with all the complex marketing plans that are needed to compete in such a high-level business, the entrepreneurial spirit still has to be kept alive underneath the surface if new markets are to be opened up, and new entrepreneurs are to be shown how to build business centres where previously there was nothing. Despite having the IEF the JMA Group are still a consultancy, and as such they need to be able to search out new business and develop existing clients on a continuous basis, and the ground rules for that remain rooted in entrepreneurial common sense.

It is when a service company is just starting out that the entrepreneurial spirit is crucial. They then have to look at ways to generate enquiries from the general marketplace, and to spread the word of their achievements and expertise among the relevant business and government communities.

One method, which has proved remarkably successful for JMA over the years is a campaign of public education, a method which Tony used from the start, and which has also been successful, albeit at a different level, for Jim Martin himself. People come to hear him speak. They are impressed by what they hear and as a result they want to hire him to consult for them, or to buy his products.

In March 1982, when he was just establishing himself in London with his brand new team, Tony started organizing courses which would attract the sort of people that he wanted to win as clients for his new company. It was a perfect way of promoting the company to a very tightly defined target market, and of generating some cashflow at the same time. The delegates to the courses happily paid for the privilege of becoming potential new business-leads, which meant that JMA's marketing campaign was actually a source of profits as well as a source of new business.

During the courses JMA consultants got to know the candidates, found out what their problems were, and made the first line of contact. Any list of delegates is, almost by definition, a list of leads since they have all shown an interest in the subject and a willingness to believe that the company giving the seminar is a reliable source of ideas and explanations. By attending a course delegates have spent at least two days being dazzled by the expertise of the speakers. It is then simply a matter of finding out whether they are in the market to buy some project work, and if so, then selling it to them.

JMA also launched a magazine called *Perspective* at the same time, which they sold on a subscription basis. The editorial was provided by Jim, Dixon, Tony or any of the consultants who had something controversial to say. Both Jim and Dixon taught some of the courses themselves. Tony started by drawing up a programme of seminars at various hotels and bought the Datamation mailing list of 17,000 names. Most of the seminars lasted for one or two days. Some of them attracted up to fifty delegates.

At the same time there are the existing seminars which Jim holds independently four or five times a year in Europe, at which Tony and his consultants again have opportunities to meet delegates and make contacts. There might be anything up to 200 senior people in the audience who have spent a large sum of money on hearing the chairman of JMA talk. They are all strong sources of potential business. The delegates can be mailed to ensure that they know that the company exists, and to explain that it practises all the things which Jim preaches, and which they have already expressed an interest in by registering. The company can offer to implement the ideas which they have heard about.

Not everyone on every course has the potential to become a customer, but it does not take an experienced salesperson long to sort out which ones have the necessary authority and the ability to become effective inside salespeople. A personal note to each one, asking if they would like to meet in the evenings after the seminars to discuss their particular problems, is one way of narrowing the field. A questionnaire can be circulated asking who else in their companies has the necessary authority, or would be interested in consulting services.

Service companies are in the business of selling 'satisfactions' as much as projects. Their salespeople have to work out what these satisfactions are for those potential clients. It may be that they want a particular technical problem solved, or they may simply want some glory and recognition within their own organizations. They might be seeking bureaucratic safety, trying to build an empire or to win promotion.

Whatever their motivation, the salespeople have to demonstrate how their services will help them to achieve their goals.

When the inside salespeople and service company salespeople have agreed on the next steps needed to bring a contract into being, they have to agree on the initial level of funding needed. It has to be low enough to gain approval, but high enough for the service company to be able to produce excellent results midway through, otherwise there will be insufficient time to arrange for add-on coverage.

The inside salespeople must fully explain their funding situations to the service company salespeople. Each one will be different and each one will be willing to fund a different amount of initial work before wanting to assess the prospects of the project.

When setting the pricing the service company has to bear in mind the value of the project to the customers. If the potential pay-off is going to be high and money is in plentiful supply, then they point these facts out to the customer, frequently.

WINNING MORE BUSINESS

BUILDING CLIENT RELATIONSHIPS

- The importance of add-on sales.
- Avoiding time-wasting speculative and competitive pitches.
- A satisfied customer is the best possible sales lead.
- It is better not to have to compete for business— you might lose.

One of the great truths in almost any industry is that it is always easier to get add-on business than new business. There are a number of reasons for this. To begin with clients always like to continue working with service companies who they have found to be dependable and trustworthy. Support from top-class service companies is one of the most effective methods by which executives can 'get things done'. Once the service company has a satisfied client company they should be able to continue winning new business from them, even if the inside salesperson changes jobs or moves to another organization.

Winning a customer for the first time is a long, arduous and often expensive process. Selling them a second, third or fourth project must be easier than going back out into the cold and starting work on selling a first project to someone else who doesn't know you from Adam. It will only be easier, of course, if the service company has managed to win the loyalty of the client.

In order to win this sort of loyalty from their customers, however, companies need to give their clients exactly what they want. That does not just mean the corporate client, but the individual as well. In most cases that means the inside salespeople. If they are to maintain long and fruitful relationships with them they always need to hold a picture of their total careers in mind, and work towards keeping them personally satisfied.

If they have a good idea of where the client wants to end up, they are more likely to be able to provide the sort of support which is needed to achieve the desired goals.

To maintain a relationship a consultant from a service company will need to keep the clients fed with new ideas for ways to expand and improve their projects. They will need to provide them with briefings and presentations that the clients can give in order to communicate the project's results within their own organization, allowing them to gain wider acceptance or more funding. All clients need a steady flow of reports, positioning papers and anything that will demonstrate to them that they are in charge of successful projects.

It would be a mistake for any service company to concentrate solely on the detailed tasks and ignore the broader issues of how to make use of the results of those tasks. When one project is over a new one has to be found to take its place. A customer who provides an increasing workload fills the gaps and allows the service company to thrive and grow. If projects make the customers successful, they are going to want to come back for more, and the service company could find that they are still working in the same building five years after a short-term project began.

To increase steadily the amount of business that comes from any one client, managers have to plan well ahead, working through the decision process in time to have the additional funds available before the current ones dry up. Lead times for money can sometimes be as much as twelve months, which means that as soon as service companies win contracts, they have to start talking to the clients about how things will develop when the initial goals have been attained.

Often, of course, the clients will be reluctant to commit themselves to anything else until they have seen how the service company will perform on the first tasks. To get over this the managers must work out two critical dates and mark them on their calendars with giant red exclamation marks. These are the dates on which they submit their next year's budgets for their projects and the sweep-up date for year-end money in the current fiscal year. Those are the times to ask for more money. If they don't ask, they won't get.

Most client companies when buying outside services will, if given a choice, ask for a request for proposal (RFP). This is little more than a 'crapshoot', and is nearly always a disaster for the service company which has done all the preliminary work on convincing a client that they need their services. Any service industry salesperson will want to avoid an RFP at all costs. In order to avoid it, however, they must explain to the inside salesperson why it would be a bad idea.

The only winners in the RFP game are the companies which cut their prices to unrealistic levels, and even they only win in the short term, since they mostly go out of business as quickly as they come in. As with everything else in the free market—you get what you pay for.

A major tenet of the procurement philosophies of most large companies is that there should be competition among contractors. The superficial sense of this from their point of view is obvious, although in reality it does not lead to them choosing the best sub-contractors for the job, or in receiving value for money.

In an ideal world the client company will precisely define what it wants to buy from the service companies, and will put the specifications out for competitive bidding. The qualified and competent company who submits the lowest bid automatically wins the business.

For the sort of project services which JMA provides, this type of approach does not work, since it is impossible to specify in advance precisely what has to be done. In many cases if the customers knew what it was that they wanted they wouldn't need to do the project at all, since they would already have the answers they needed without paying other people to tell them. It is the same as asking for quotes from a doctor, a lawyer or a tax accountant. It is a gross waste of time and money.

A highly placed US government official who was about to put out a 'moose call' for proposals was once asked by Tony Carter 'If it was your money would you do it this way?' He answered,

> Of course not. If it was my money I would give you the job at the price you quoted, since it seems like a reasonable price and I am positive you can perform. You would also have finished the job by the time we can prepare an RFP and go through the full competitive procurement cycle. Furthermore, it will probably cost me more to put together the RFP than I could possibly save. Still

> I have no choice, I must go through the complete cycle, even
> through it may not be in the government's best interest.

Sometimes service companies can believe they are on the inside track
for winning a project and will suddenly find that things are moving
towards an RFP. The mistake they might make is to assume that because
they are on the inside track they will automatically win. In fact their
chances of success are virtually nil. By that point in the proceedings
the inside salespeople are already quite familiar with the favoured
consultancy's ideas and plans, so much so that they probably now believe
that they are their own. When the proposals come in from the competition
they will see that all the fresh ideas are coming from other people, not
from the familiar company.

The most sensible way for a client to procure services from companies
like JMA is to first decide how much should be invested in a project.
Having set the budget the client can then select a company who can
maximize the output which can be obtained from the budget. The
difficulty is in finding executives in client organizations who are both
able and willing to adapt the procurement regulations of their companies
in order to achieve this.

One of the most common delusions of people who habitually go in
for RFP 'crapshoots' is that they 'almost won the last one'. Because
the customers have tried to avoid hurting the feelings of the losers, they
have told them all that they 'nearly won'. To believe such a statement
is pure self-delusion and a successful service company cannot afford
the time to be chasing up so many outside chances. The simple
percentages are against anyone who enters one of these competitive races.
There are also bound to be a few companies who underquote through
ignorance, desperation or deviousness. Any company that wins on price
has almost certainly undercut the undercutters, and has therefore made
a serious pricing error and will be unable to deliver the goods.

Once a target has been selected at JMA, the consultants will go through
a lot of tedious and painstaking research, writing and rehearsing before
going in to sell. There is never any point in going to talk to a potential
client unless they know everything there is to know about their situation,
their problems and the ways in which the company might be able to
help. That research can sometimes mean talking to outside organizations
about the target organization, particularly suppliers. If a sales team has
just managed to win a large order for computer hardware to the target
customer, for instance, they are likely to be very keen to talk about
it. They will be a mine of useful information to a consultant who needs

to know what sort of problems the target customer is likely to be facing.

If a service company is very lucky, it will receive an order from this first call. The second best chance is to be asked to put forward a proposal for dealing with a particular problem which the client has. The third likely outcome is that the company will be told that they will be kept on file and called in if anything suitable comes up. The worst is to be told that the client has no requirement for such services and is never likely to have any.

The first three answers all hold out hope to a service company, as long as the required proposal is not in competition with someone who practically has the business already. If the prospect thinks they might be interested at a later date, then they can go on to the trapline, and be drip-fed information about the company and what it is doing. The fourth answer simply shows that the salesperson got either the targeting or the presentation wrong.

The golden rules for all service industry salespeople from then on are to abandon sinking ships immediately, or else they will pull everyone to the bottom with them, and to keep after potential winners with dogged persistence.

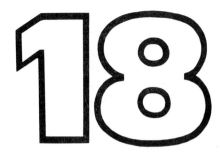

THE WINNING FORMULA

- Keeping the balance between sales, recruitment, management and profit and loss.

- Keeping the family atmosphere.

- If you don't want to win then you aren't in the race.

- If people aren't enjoying their jobs they should be working somewhere else.

- Mixing business and pleasure isn't enough—doing business must *be* a pleasure.

During his reign at JMA, Tony Carter's office bristled with mementoes and pictures from the rugby field, and many of the other managers and associates of the company shared his enthusiasms for sport. He encouraged a clubhouse atmosphere, and talked continuously in sporting metaphors. The growth of JMA has, as a result, been rather like the rise of a football team to stardom.

Every sport is all about winning, and most successful companies also look upon 'winning' as the main goal. There are different ways of winning, of course, but all of them involve the pursuit of excellence in various ways.

All managers in a successful consultancy are seen to be in competition all the time, whether they like it or not, even if they are only competing with themselves and with the goals which they set themselves. Without the spark of competition they would not be able to survive in a business where money has to be earned every day. It is not like working for some giant bureacratic machine which somehow survives through the lean periods with no noticeable change of pace. Workers in a service company must always be aware of their targets, their bottom line and the fact that if they don't win new business today then there will be no work for them to do tomorrow. They need to remain flexible and be ready to alter course the moment there are signs of trouble.

In order to be a high achiever in the service world people need to know and understand themselves and their company intimately. They need to understand clearly what it is that the team does well, and about ways in which performance can be improved. Self-knowledge is a vital ingredient in any sustained success story, if you don't know what you are capable of, how can you achieve anything?

At the same time they also need the vision and understanding of the world beyond the company's own frontiers—a feeling for the present and future events which must shape the company's destiny. No company works in a vacuum, they are all subject to the economic and political movements around the world. People will have more or less money to spend as a result of outside circumstances, a sales message has to be tailored to fit the ever-changing circumstances, or a company becomes outdated and soon dies.

The latter is particularly true of a service company like JMA, who need to be at the leading edge of technology all the time if they are to serve their customers. That means seeing what is coming, and making sure that they are part of it. With a technical team of the calibre of JMA's there is never a shortage of technical knowledge, the challenge is to recognize which bits are going to be significant and to turn what could be just a greater potential workload into an ongoing and growing commercial success story. This requires a broader vision, plus the right management skills.

So the survival of a service company in the marketplace depends on the skills of its managers and technicians in a number of business areas. They need to be able to sell, to manage people, projects and money, and they need to be able to manage growth.

Without the initial sale nothing happens, but just selling is not enough. If the product or service is sold wrongly, then the consultants will be unable to deliver to the client whatever he wanted or needed to buy. A good salesperson might be able to sell something to a customer once, but if the product doesn't live up to the promises which have been made on its behalf, the customer will not be coming back for more. A really great salesperson makes sure that the product is exactly what the customer needs, and then explains convincingly why this is so, secure in the knowledge that the customer's experience with the product will bear out promises.

Next come the people and the projects. Without people or projects to manage the company does not exist so recruitment and project management are vital. Equally, without profits or growth the company has no future and everyone has to be aware of the bottom line and of how targets have to be met or exceeded.

To manage these disparate elements is a juggling act. The targets must be ambitious but attainable, otherwise people will become demotivated and discouraged when they fail to achieve them. The people must also see a benefit from the state of the bottom line. If the company makes a healthy profit, then they need to see that directly reflected in their paychecks.

The final measure of whether or not a company is winning is the bottom line, or P/L. The P/L is the very small difference between two large numbers, revenue and costs. Both sets of numbers need to be watched constantly if they are to be prised far enough apart to reach corporate objectives for growth.

Pricing is a very delicate subject in all service industries. While companies have to be competitive in their quotes, they also have to be constantly aware that if they don't charge enough for their services they will not be able to hire the best people, or to put as much work in on the clients' problems as they should. It is always easy to cut prices in order to win business, it is not always as easy to find the right rate for the job which is realistic for both sides of the deal.

When clients stay with a service company for a number of years, there are going to be times when the prices have to be raised, not only because of general rises in costs, but because the service which the company is offering will be improving all the time as it grows, and will consequently be worth more to the customers.

A service company therefore needs to plan its price rises well ahead, and must ensure that the client knows that they are coming, and understands why they are necessary. If the client is happy with the way things are going, and feels that the rises are fair, there will be no problem.

Sometimes the rise will be caused by the promotion of one or more key people on the project team. If the client is as happy with their work as their employers are, then the client will not object to such key people receiving a just reward for their labours. But the client must be able to understand what the money is for.

The largest costs in the consultancy industry are people-related, and yet some consultants feel shy about charging them on at the market rate. It is obvious that the consultants have to be charged out directly, since that is the purpose of the business.

A consultancy that wants to attract the best people has to err on the generous side when it comes to salary increases and other people-related costs. If they are mean about them they will have an unhappy ship. If they don't plan them effectively there will be a lot of lost money, lost effort and lost people with all the subsequent replacement costs and low morale.

Everyone who works at JMA is in demand in the marketplace. They all know their value, and they have to be treated fairly.

Time is the way in which a consultancy weighs its product, like a greengrocer uses his scales for each transaction, a consultancy must ensure that they keep an accurate check on the quantities of time which they are selling. Strict time records are therefore kept and are relayed promptly to the accounts department. Late submissions are frowned on since they always lead to missed payments, and might even become forgotten by a busy consultant, leading to lost revenue.

Each new project gives a consultancy the opportunity to expand their staff. An employee, whether freelance or full-time, gives twice as much profit and opportunity to the consultancy. If project A requires an extra consultant, and there is enough money in the project's budget to pay for the position, then any income that consultant can generate by working on projects B or C at the same time will go straight to the bottom line. In a people business, people must be treated fairly, which means clients and employees alike.

The senior management at JMA like to keep the family atmosphere alive. Many companies like to boast that they are 'people businesses', but when the managers are showing anyone around the premises they spend most of the time talking about their marvellous machinery, and completely ignoring the people. In the service industry, where people are the prime asset of the company, it is doubly important that this doesn't happen. If people are to work well and stay with a consultancy they have to feel that they belong, that they are valued and that they are part of a family.

The management at JMA are all well aware that as the company grows larger it becomes harder to remember where you came from, unless you make a conscious effort to retain the original corporate philosophy, upon which everything else has been built.

Tony Carter's style of management was by far the strongest influence on the company during its formative years. Not only did he believe in mixing his business and pleasure, he actually believed that business is a pleasure, and that work and play are indivisible in a balanced lifestyle. As a result he believed in involving the families of his colleagues in the business process, if they want to. It goes back to the fundamental belief that if people aren't having fun they probably aren't working effectively.

The philosophy of involving families starts at the top. Each year JMA takes the country managers off for a few days of planning meetings, somewhere a long way from the office like Portugal or Biarritz. Families are included in the package and each day a different sector of the business comes up for discussion. By choosing exotic locations JMA rewards the families as well as the employees, and gives them a chance to find out better what it is that people working within JMA actually do when they are away from home.

After the business session the families get together for meals and other social activities. The result is a team which understands better the ramifications of everything they do. They understand what makes their fellow directors tick, and they form bonds which couldn't be formed simply during working hours. The country managers then take the same principles and apply them to the next layer of management.

Although the company expects dedication and hard work from its employees, it does not expect its people to be workaholics. Most consultants are at the age where they are also bringing up families and expecting to enjoy the fruits of hard work put in earlier in their careers. Any employer who makes too many demands on his people, enforcing long partings from families or endless late nights and early mornings, is going to end up with over-tired and disillusioned people. No one can function well without a good balance of working and private lives.

The first of the international planning sessions which Cor Swart, the Dutch director, attended was in a beautiful mountain hotel outside Oslo. He remembers flying out on a Sunday evening in summer to have a meeting with Tony. He arrived at the hotel to be told that Tony had changed his plane and would be out the next day. The following morning, sitting beside a mountain river in the sun, waiting for his new boss to arrive, he reflected on how different his new life was from the old planning meetings of his previous employer, ICL, with its strict rituals and performance measurement techniques. At the JMA meetings the managers find that their time is freed from the everyday interruptions of the office, and they are able to concentrate clearly on the future and where they are heading.

This 'family' approach to employee relations is carried right through the company. Every individual who joins JMA undergoes continuous career development, and profit-sharing is a major part of everyone's remuneration package. In 1987, for instance, the total bonus allocated to employees amounted to more than $300,000.

If a company is to be successful it must agree to share the proceeds of that success with the people who are needed to make it happen. Around 18 per cent of the equity in JMA belongs to employees below director level.

Good consultants are balanced, happy people who feel good about themselves, their employers and their employers' products. Only by creating an environment in which this can happen, can a company hope to thrive.

FAST FORWARD INTO THE FUTURE

- Changing gear from 'profit-making', to planning and investing for growth.
- Building an accurate picture of the future and then planning how to make it work.
- The story so far is only about the laying of foundation stones. The most extraordinary things are yet to come — for JMA and for every other business which intends to survive in the future.

'CASE is like teenage sex,' points out one of JMA's senior managers. 'Everyone is talking about it, some of them are trying it, but no one is doing it very well yet.'

The analogy is a good one. It is an immature marketplace but, just like sex, when it matures it is going to be big. Behind CASE there are a number of new technologies which are as ripe for the market as CASE was a few years ago. The seeds have been sown and the crops are beginning to show through the ground. Soon the companies who have positioned themselves right will be able to reap a fabulous series of harvests.

Through its connections with Jim Martin, JMA has been able to come in at the beginning of an industry which is likely to be one of the biggest and most profitable boom areas of the next decade. Like many fledgling industries based on good ideas and requiring major changes in traditional thinking, it is taking longer to establish itself than the pioneers might have hoped, but that is always the way. At the consumer end, we just have to look at how long we were all talking about video recorders, personal computers and mobile telephones before they started to become a reality in the marketplace. The pioneer companies which manage to survive the lean early years of a new industry are the ones in the best position to thrive in the boom years.

There were many critics of Tony Carter's style of management, and there were those who believed in the beginning that many of his dreams were just that, and could never be translated into a solid reality. There were a lot of mistakes made along the way, but there were also some good, far-sighted decisions. In the end a company can only be judged on its profitability, and by 1989 JMA was one of the fastest growing information technology companies in the world, if you discount those which grow through acquisition.

In 1986 the company's revenue was just over £6 million, the following year they grew to over £10.5 million. In 1988 that figure had nearly doubled to over £19 million, and looked set to continue at that rate.

The pre-tax profits for the company during that period rose from £29,000 to £1.5 million and the pre-tax earnings per share rose from £0.03 to £1.23. The number of employees in the group rose from about 20 in 1982 to 300 in 1988.

By the end of his reign, however, the other directors believed Tony was concentrating too heavily on short-term profits. They believed there were many more things that JMA could and should be doing in order to grow into a really substantial company, but these things required investment.

Tony had not, for instance, been willing to put money into creating products which JMA would wholly own and would be able to sell. Ian Palmer was particularly keen that they should be doing more research and development in that area, but as long as Tony was in charge the funds were being turned on and off whenever he felt money was tight. With the increased interest from Jim Martin, and with David Fairbairn taking over from Tony, the whole emphasis of the company's management style changed. Whereas before Tony had always worked to keep things simple, as they had been at the beginning, David, Jim and the other directors felt able to plan a more complex and sophisticated organization. They were able to move forward from the 'seat-of-the-pants', tactical management style which had launched the company, to a more strategic and long-term plan.

One spin-off is that there is now a sympathetic atmosphere for research and development, although still strictly controlled by the demands of the marketplace. The fear among the operating companies was that an R&D department might be allowed to become an ivory tower, divorced from reality. To ensure that doesn't happen, David is insisting that any R&D project can only happen if there has been a definite statement from the 'sharp end' of the company, where the consultants and salespeople are actually meeting the clients and know the problems of the marketplace, which lays out the potential benefits and drawbacks of undertaking that work.

By the time Tony stepped down from being CEO the company was already a substantial multinational corporation, but it was not behaving like one. It was still behaving like a small start-up operation. They were not, for instance, spending much money on market research or other scientific approaches to marketing. That had to change. At the same time, the executive committee did not want to destroy the entrepreneurial spirit which Tony had fostered. They did not want to take on the negative aspects of large company philosophy, which might render it too rigid to permit innovation or creativity to exist. They believed it was critical that the company retained its imaginativeness and opportunism. They decided that the Country Manager is King philosophy was no longer appropriate. Although the various territories should continue to work in the same way as they were doing before, there should be international 'streams' of expertise benefiting from synergy and shared experiences.

The directors decided that they must look at what the company was doing more closely and break it down into three streams, which would each have leaders who would be responsible for all activities in that product area, wherever in the world they were happening. The stream manager would then be on an equal footing to the territory or 'country' manager. Firstly there was the consulting business, secondly the IEF sales and consulting which Texas Instruments were now beginning to see as a major new business for them, and thirdly a new concept which had been exciting both Ian Palmer and Jim for some time—packaged expertise.

Packaging expertise basically means turning the knowledge which the consultants hold in their heads and in their various information deposits, into marketable products which will be of use to as wide a range of clients as possible. In a way the IEF is a magnificent piece of packaged expertise, as are Jim's books or the methodology handbooks, but there are many other areas where the concept will work just as effectively. Hypermedia, which the JMA people in the US had been working on under Ian's auspices, will provide just one way of packaging and presenting fantastic amounts of information in a user-friendly form.

Right at the beginning, the company was founded on the packaged expertise of the information engineering methodology which was originated by Jim and then packaged by disciplined minds like Ian Palmer and Ian MacDonald. What made the early JMA companies different from other consultancies was that there actually was an underlying product and 'way of doing things', which entrepreneurs like Cor Swart and Shaun Boyle could go out and sell and practice. Because the methodology was so logical it was easy for new people to absorb it and practise it. Without that the business would only have been as successful as each individual consultant on each particular job, it would not have been able to grow into anything substantial. Some of the entrepreneurs, such as Cor, would then do other things as well as working with the methodology, such as telecommunications consulting, but in time it became evident that the most profitable way to work was with a formal and logical structure, because of the opportunities this affords for add-on business.

If a consultancy is merely solving problems for clients as they occur, the value of the service is down-graded. If you can solve problems and also leave behind the capacity for clients to solve problems for themselves next time, through written material, training or software, you suddenly have a product which is worth far more to clients.

Because the fundamental methods of the company have been well documented, firstly in Jim's books and videos and then in the methodology handbooks, there has been a high degree of conformity in the way they work all over the world, even if the commercial structures differed in Tony's organization.

A company which has built its reputation on being at the leading edge of new technology has to ensure that it stays in that position, and does not allow itself to become complacent. That means keeping up with everything that is going on in the world of technology, keeping a broad picture in mind and being able to see what the changes all add up to.

In many ways JMA has become a corporate version of Jim Martin himself. Both have access at the highest levels of a number of different companies and organizations which are doing exciting things in the worlds of technology. As a result they are able to cross-fertilize ideas, providing greater degrees of experience, and judgements based on deeper understandings of the way the world is going.

In the end the continuing success of an organization like JMA is based on the knowledge which they are able to acquire, comprehend and communicate to others.

One of the major aims of the JMA consultants is skills transfer, which means teaching the clients to be self-sufficient. If that happens, the consultancy would be in danger of teaching itself out of business, unless it can be sure that it is learning new things at a faster rate than it is teaching them.

As technology becomes more complex, someone needs to simplify it, automate it and make it more user-friendly. If you look at the cockpit of an early fighter jet you are confronted with a dazzling array of dials and knobs. Very few people were actually skilful enough to fly the planes safely. Now, with the help of technology they have been 'de-skilled', so that pilots need to concentrate on little more than a screen, a stick and a couple of pedals, because the machine will do it all for them.

Management software is in the same position as the early jets, each refinement leads to another complication for the user to learn to handle. While we now have the technology to achieve much of what we want, we lack the people skilled enough to operate it. The software must continue to be dramatically simplified so that a lower level of skill is required to operate it.

The problem is that most of the best knowledge is inside the heads of the individual consultants who have actually worked with clients on their problems. Ways have to be found of capturing the knowledge inside these few heads and packaging it for wider distribution. If the consultancy can just find a way of capturing that knowledge and expertise and packaging it in a way that makes it accessible to others, it will be able to increase its own learning curve and, with any luck, end up with a package which it can sell.

This process Jim Martin calls 'encapsulating knowledge'. In the good old days it was done by writing reports or books, which contained all the relevant ideas and solutions. Now, particularly in the high-technology fields, there is simply too much data for that to be practical. If all the consultants in JMA wrote down all the knowledge which they have on their subject, no one would have time to read it all. The answer lies in software vehicles which will make information available in volume, allowing the learners to follow threads and thought processes selectively.

Martin has designed a 'hypermedia' product which, once again, his late-night programmer friends prototyped in Bermuda. The product, called MediaBrain, was designed to capture complex knowledge and make it accessible. The prototype of MediaBrain was programmed by Alan Littleford, a software artist who seemed to be existing on a cerebral plane as remote from daily life as a computer simulation is from reality. He is a mathematical and musical genius, his head filled with the bizarre logic of science-fiction worlds.

The idea of MediaBrain is to take the knowledge which Martin and his colleagues carry in their heads and build it into computers, so that others can learn and build on it. It is like providing roadmaps for the mind, making massive amounts of knowledge digestible and usable.

JMA is now involved in major projects all over the world. In Holland, for instance, the company was able to advise the Dutch government on the setting up of an electronic mail system. The EEC was building an internal system with the idea that all European countries would be able to link into it. JMA suggested to the Dutch government that they should study the question on their behalf, and the consultants came up with the suggestion that the EEC system was too complex, but that there were already similar systems up and running in places like Canada which they could link into. They were only able to take on an assignment like this because of their overview of the various different industries involved.

Through his contacts with the industry, and the models he builds from the information that he gathers, Jim Martin is able to make useful predictions about the way technology and business will develop. JMA, as a company, are now in a similar position. They have their fingers on the pulse of so many different companies in so many different countries that they can make observations based on hard logic about what is coming.

Whether it is connected with optical fibres, microchips or the fact that by 1995 some desktop computers will be as powerful as the most powerful mainframe computer is in 1990, they can look at what is happening and work out the probability figures.

There are exciting developments under way in superconductivity, for instance, in the development of new types of chips and neural computers, in the marriage of television and computer technologies, and in broadband telecommunications.

Not only can a consultancy like JMA predict developments, they can also see the resulting social and managerial consequences. If, for instance, the developments in desktop computing happen as predicted, anyone with a terminal will have immense power at their fingertips. Huge slices of middle-management are going to become as redundant as farmworkers with the advent of agricultural machinery. Companies need to be warned of these likely changes so that they can prepare themselves and their people for them.

Within twenty years there will be as few people working in

manufacturing as there are in agriculture (agriculture once employed half America's working population, it now employs about 2 per cent, but the production of food has risen enormously). If society is to plan for these changes, to make them as painless as possible, it must be able to predict them, and understand what they mean.

To help them with the gathering of the necessary knowledge, JMA launched a 20/20 telecommunications study in 1989 to examine the future developments in telecommunications networks and services over the next thirty years, which will have a direct impact on the competitive operation and profitability of corporations. It is another example of packaged expertise.

The study is being sponsored by corporations all over the world who want to know the answers to a number of key questions. Many of them are also choosing to participate in the study itself, which will give them access to the research findings and conclusions prior to the official publication of the report. Jim Martin launched the project personally, and it has taken off faster than any of them expected, with big companies around the world keen to participate. Everyone wants a crystal ball to tell them what is likely to happen next. They all know that, as Martin consistently points out, there is really no such thing as a crystal ball. What there is, however, is a massive amount of knowledge which, if pulled together and structured, gives a clear idea of what is likely to happen in the years ahead.

For many years Jim has maintained his own personal model of the future, which he uses for analysing the major trends in telecommunications and information technology, assessing the impact of emerging technologies on corporations and society in general. The 20/20 study will broaden this model with masses of new information, gleaned from the brightest people in the sponsoring organizations. The more information that goes into the model the greater the likely insight into the future.

Rather than just looking at developments in technology, the results will give organizations predictions about their specific industries and companies, based on in-depth research and analysis. By understanding what is happening in the technology laboratories today, it will be possible to determine when the changes are likely to reach the marketplace, based on known lead-times. By using cold logic to work out the lead-times for future changes, a jigsaw emerges which, when pieced together, gives a valuable picture of what is to come.

What is already certain is that the speed of change is going to increase rapidly. Companies that do not keep up are almost certain to go out of business faster than in the past. Recent history has already demonstrated this. When you look at how slowly the world changed up until the last hundred years, and then look at how much has changed in the last twenty years, you can see how the effects are becoming cumulative, snowballing beyond anything currently comprehended by the majority of executives. With the help of computers we can benefit from the cumulative knowledge. We can benefit from all the experience which exists everywhere. If entire libraries of law books can be brought down to a computer on a lawyer's desk and the computer can search for precedents, the lawyer will be able to work far better. The same feats are possible in all knowledge-based industries, everyone who has access to greater knowledge will be able to improve their working and decision-making abilities greatly.

The 20/20 study started by looking at the core technologies and what is happening in the laboratories. From that it examined what machines are likely to be built and when. Once you know what the machines are going to look like you can start to work out the possible applications which they could be used for in everything from education to medicine, banking to agriculture, manufacturing to government.

By working with a number of specific industry groups such as banks and airlines, the creators of the models are able to see how each will change and how those changes will impact upon other sectors.

The final stage will be to analyse how all these changes will effect society. Will it lead to mass prosperity or mass unemployment? How can companies ensure that they are building their human potential at the same speed as their technological potential? All the new technology will be useless if there is no one able or willing to use it.

There have been innumerable, expensive business failures in the past, nearly always made because people did not have enough information with which to make accurate predictions. A company might sink hundreds of millions of dollars into developing a new product, when a future model would have told them that developments in rival technologies would render the product obsolete almost immediately. Such mistakes may be avoided, or at least be minimized, by using a detailed future model.

By being able to model the future more clearly, companies will be able to recognize strategic opportunities which would only have been inspired guesswork in the past, using their technology as a competitive weapon.

The most senior levels of management are likely to be a large market for the high-technology industries in the coming years, simply because they are so badly served with tools at the moment. While companies like JMA have no trouble talking to information systems and data processing executives, and in constructing systems which will be useful to them, there is much that still needs to be done to provide the very top levels of management with decision-making support.

Top executives have a lot of questions to which they need answers. Where, for instance, should they locate a new factory or warehouse? What product mix should they be aiming for? These are probably the most important questions which can be asked in any company, and any information system which can provide better answers will be worth its weight in gold.

Senior managers are a massive potential market for consultancies and software companies who are looking far enough into the future. At the moment the industry is selling systems which give clients the competitive edge on their day-to-day decision-making and management tasks. But what happens when all companies have the same or similar systems? The first brewer who bought a fleet of delivery lorries to replace his dray horses had a considerable competitive advantage. Owning a fleet of lorries would no longer be considered an advantage to a modern brewery, it is a daily necessity, so they have to look for more sophisticated ways of getting ahead.

It won't be long before all major companies have information systems which make them competitive, and the top of the management triangle will be the next place to look for technological improvement. The work which JMA are doing with hypermedia should give them the leverage which they need to break into this potential market. The research for the 20/20 study is helping them to open the doors to senior managers' offices, allowing them to introduce themselves to a sector of the market which has until now been relatively ignorant of the high-technology market, but which could soon be at the heart of it.

The major thrust of the 20/20 study will be towards looking at telecommunications technology. Telecommunications is in a period of revolutionary change. The attendant developments have the potential to change the fabric of society. Emerging products and services will not only serve the public and corporate services market, but will also change the nature of corporations themselves.

The most obvious example of an early result of telecommunications developments has been in the financial world. Global networks have created a global economy. Billions of dollars in the form of bits of information are transmitted around the world in seconds. A financial dealer in New York can operate 24 hours a day; as the market in London closes, New York opens, and as New York closes, Tokyo opens, and so on in an almost continuous loop. Anyone in the financial industry who could have predicted such developments a year earlier than the competition would have been able to execute pre-emptive competitive attacks.

There are likely to be many more such opportunities in the future, and the people who manage to predict them first will have a head start in the race to exploit them. As more and more companies join into the study, the model gets richer and richer, with more facts being poured into it from all over the world. The consultants then have to structure all the information, building links and paths through it, creating scenarios for clients, assessing the impact on individual companies and answering their questions.

As the number of high-capacity communications channels available to all sectors of business increases, so do the opportunities. Just as the opening up of new sea lanes in the sixteenth and seventeenth centuries established the early foundations of an international system of trading goods, communications networks have opened up new international markets for the trade in information. Corporations of all sizes benefit from improved communications. Networks of computers linking remote offices to a corporate centre enable improvements in productivity to be made through the better management of resources. The networks which interlink the various parts of a corporation change the structure of decision-making, potentially diminishing bureaucracy, and replacing it with a structure which is dynamic and responsive to change. Consequently, new linkages with other corporations are provided, changing entire industry structures and opening up new business opportunities for existing corporations.

With dramatically increased communication channel capacity, new products and new services will emerge. New products will not only enter the domestic consumer markets, but also change the public and corporate service markets as well as corporations themselves. These new products will bring about at first subtle, then major changes in the way we conduct our lives, both at home and at work.

In the past, corporate telecommunications were viewed as a necessary but expensive overhead. That attitude is changing and telecommunications at the beginning of the 1990s and in the future is likely to be perceived as a competitive weapon, fundamental to the whole existence of corporations, and a principal means of achieving higher levels of profitability.

Traditional attitudes to the nature of work will have to change, and people and organizations which lack the imagination to grasp the future will be the casualties of the revolution.

The 20/20 project acts as a profit earner for JMA, while at the same time ensuring that they reinforce their position at the leading edge of their industry. Although primarily looking at the telecommunications field, the results will impact on every area of technology and the future.

The 20/20 model gives JMA the ability to reach from top management, examining strategic opportunities and doing enterprise engineering, to IS management with information engineering, down to implementation of systems with RAD (rapid application development) techniques. This gives the company three thrusts, each different in their nature and each complementary to the others. In combination they give the ability to help a client company rethink its strategic opportunities, retool its IS organization, put into place the infrastructure for the more effective information systems, and build systems of high quality at high speed.

It is interesting to observe that the last decade of a century often sets the pattern for the next century. The last decade of the eighteenth century brought the invention of the steamship and the development of factory machinery using the steam engine. This set the pattern for the industrial growth of the nineteenth century.

The last decade of the nineteenth century brought the invention of the motor car, radio and telephone networks, setting the pattern for the twentieth century.

The 1990s are bringing optical fibres and broadband information networks, optical disks, high-definition television in which television and computer technology converge, the automation of factories, genetic engineering, the growth of energy-saving small technology and attention to 'greening' the environment. The style for the twenty-first century is being set—a century when corporations and institutions will be worldwide, knowledge industries will predominate, mankind's vast and growing knowledge will be at our fingertips and computers with artificial intelligence will pervade the fabric of our life.

JMA is setting the style for the twenty-first century corporation.